A Journey of Revelation

and Self-Discovery

A Journey of Revelation

and Self-Discovery

*A Story Unfolding, A Life Becoming, A Truth Revealing,
A Destiny Unveiling, A Song Unending*

ROGER T. BERG

Park Point
PRESS

573 Park Point Drive
Golden, Colorado 80401-7042

Park Point Press
573 Park Point Drive
Golden, Colorado 80401-7402

Scenic photographs © Joyce Berg (pages v, 120, 122)

Cover Design/Book Layout
Maria Robinson–Designs On You, LLC.
www.DesignsOnYou.weebly.com

Printed in the United States of America
Published November 2019

ISBN paperback: 978-0-917849-81-7
ISBN ebook: 978-0-917849-82-4

To family in its broadest meaning —

my immediate family and all those who

have come into my life and become family to me.

Prologue

The Journey Begins

"Your beliefs become your thoughts.

Your thoughts become your words.

Your words become your actions.

Your actions become your habits.

Your habits become your values.

Your values become your destiny."

— MAHATMA GANDHI

here was no preconceived plan to put these affirmations out into the light of public view as a salable work product. And that, as it turned out, was to be its best feature as an original piece of work, created over approximately one and a half years, embedded among my notes from my practice of reading, recording, and reflecting on the Daily Guides in the Science of Mind *monthly magazine.*

Without thought of their commercial significance, these personal affirmations flowed freely and smoothly as they followed the path of my creative thinking each day and moved me to write them just as they came to me. My only motivation for preserving them was that I felt they were a good reflection of the state of my mind, heart, and soul, my feelings, my deeper motivations, and, as I discovered on closer scrutiny by searching within, what surfaced was a precise and accurate reflection of my value system and personal themes that rule my thoughts and my way of living, teaching moments, and leaps of learning about myself.

All this deep discovery process occurred long after the original affirmations work had been created. Upon reflection, I have come to acknowledge them in awe and profound gratitude as a personal renaissance period when I was alive with receptivity to my highest order thinking.

Now they are an invitation to you to abide with me through these pages sincerely offered, to step through the portal of possibilities they may present, to gaze together at the wonders of our brightest stars, to celebrate our humanity together, to dream the dreams that are possible, to reflect on where we might fit in the lexicon of opportunities, possibilities, and our potential to serve the wider world.

I stand in awe and admiration of all of you who are now serving with meaningful intention and high purpose all those souls in our midst who are most vulnerable and in most need of our gifts and talents. You are already on this perfect path of answering your heart's calling, which I am just beginning to understand and to follow for myself. I am honored if any part of what follows ignites your interest and imagination or quietly resonates responsively to move you to a different place of how you look at the world around you and perhaps moves you affirmatively in new and exciting directions.

D e c l a r a t i o n

o f   P e r s o n a l   V a l u e s

d i s c o v e r y   o f   s e l f

HUMANISM DRIVES MY PURPOSE TO SERVICE and gives meaning to my life. Wisdom and knowledge lay deep within my giftedness and talent to give my right work impact in the wider world. I work not only because I have confidence in my abilities but because I am strongly guided and supported by something greater than myself.

My intention to serve humanity powerfully motivates me to be available and on call every day of my life, and I carry this responsibility squarely on my shoulders. I experience gratitude for being chosen to serve and, in so serving, love permeates all that I am and all that I do, and blesses me with feelings of self-worth and usefulness. All other values I carry within me supplement, augment, enhance, enlarge, and contribute to my mission, my purpose, and my destiny.

A powerful portal that places me in the midst of my right work is having the freedom and creativity to demonstrate how looking at things differently can be eminently a teaching experience, a learning opportunity, and a magical moment of being in places I've never before seen or experienced. And at each step of progress in my self-discovery, I have felt elements of courage, faith, purpose, and intention sometimes coinciding, sometimes coming on me separately or all together, at a plodding, peripatetic pace or rushing through me laser-focused toward some clearly defined goal.

Signposts have appeared along my path that helped me to take pride in my past achievements, to reevaluate my purpose, and to adjust my intentional living going forward, more clearly aligning with my authentic self and refocusing my reason for being here.

My Life Themes

and Values

my authentic self

RECURRING THEMES AND UNDERLYING VALUES that have given meaning and purpose to my life and which I celebrate and admire in others . . . all coming to me as paths to follow, lessons to be learned, gifts to be revealed . . . all creating the perfect path to my greater self-fulfillment, illuminating who I am by what I value, what I esteem, and what I hold in high regard as it comes through me or shines forth through the actions of others.

Personal Themes
That Have Formed a Mosaic of My Life

VALUES	IMAGINATION	SELF-IMAGE
CREATIVITY	STRENGTHS	INSIGHTS
DESTINY	ASPIRATIONS	WEAKNESSES
BELIEFS	ACHIEVEMENTS	POSITIVITY

COMPASSION   SPIRITUALITY   TRANSFORMATION

MINISTRY   PROPENSITIES   PURPOSE

COURAGE   INCLINATIONS

Values I Admire, Aspire to,
And Believe In as They Have Been Revealed to Me

SOLITUDE   CREATIVITY   GENEROSITY

SOCIABILITY   DEDICATION   LEGACY

COMMUNITY   FLEXIBILITY   HUMANISM

EMPATHY   CHARITY   SIMPLICITY

COOPERATION   CONFIDENCE   HEALTH

LOYALTY   GIFTEDNESS   TRUTHFULNESS

ENTHUSIASM   SERVANT LEADERSHIP   PRAISE

RELIABILITY   HOPEFULNESS   WORTHINESS

RESPONSIBILITY   FAITH   NON-JUDGMENT

SINCERITY   PATIENCE   INTENTION

RESPECT   FAIRNESS   FAMILY

LOVE   LIGHTHEARTEDNESS   POSITIVITY

INTEGRITY   SERVICE   AUTHENTICITY

CONGRUITY   LITERACY   GRATITUDE

KNOWLEDGE   USEFULNESS   SPIRITUALITY

WISDOM   SELF-WORTH   PURPOSE

FREEDOM   ONENESS

Contents

CHAPTER 1

Humanity

Casting a Wider Presence in the World

"I will not die an unlived life. I will not live in fear of falling or catching fire. I choose to inhabit my days, to allow my living to open me, to make me less afraid, more accessible; to loosen my heart until it becomes a wing, a torch, a promise. I choose to risk my significance, to live so that which came to me as seed goes to the next as blossom, and that which came to me as blossom goes on as fruit."

— DAWNA MARKOVA

i n t r o d u c t i o n

h u m a n i t y

I imagine myself poised above the Earth at 30,000 feet, looking down on the outlines of continents, vast oceans, land formations, and mountainous regions, imagining the population centers, the scattered rural habitations, believing and seeing all that lies below me in a unified image, without cracks or crevices, no struggle or strife, no wars or violence, life ongoing, seamlessly woven into a mosaic of humanity of wholeness, of Oneness, of peace and tranquility in a world of *Namaste* where all live in harmony. I envision four contemplative spirits hovering at this elevated position above the Earth, and they might be saying:

Spirit One: *"This is where I imagine God would be."*

Spirit Two: *"Looking down on Earth just like this."*

Spirit Three: *"Incredible!"*

Spirit Four: *"Where is God, anyway?"*

Humanity is my strongest, most persistent personal value, calling me to leave behind all judgments, preconceptions, predispositions, past experiences, notions of conditional love, and now step out in faith, with high intention, gratitude for being available here and now to offer my gifts, taking the high road and answering the call to sacred service and finding the face of God in the eyes of everyone I meet. And in this way I find the answer to where God is.

As I look back and start to reconstruct the story of my life, I see people, places, and situations that now stand out as shining images of how I was directed and who was doing the directing.

All around me have been quite ordinary-appearing folks, living out their lives, and somehow our paths crossed and we touched, soul to soul, leaving an indelible impression on my personhood, forming a piece of the "me" going forward. So today I see myself made up of my core personality, a friendly and familiar inner man-child, augmented, supplemented, energized, challenged by, celebrated with, cried with . . . the souls who have come into my life, some gone, some still staying on because our work together is not yet done . . . and now the "me" who stands before the world moves ever onward and upward, becoming a stepping stone for others, as I have been able to reach higher and farther because I am standing on the shoulders of those who have gone before me and have given me the best parts of themselves.

I stand among my brothers and sisters, some wayward, some saintly, most just ordinary souls, with their virtues and their foibles—I embrace them all knowing that I need their humanity to be alive in my own life. Some of the paths that I may be led on are slippery slopes and treacherous to negotiate, so I pick and choose carefully, not always wisely, but at the end of the day, I return to being comfortable in my own skin, giving myself permission to have made mistakes, but then I move on down my path, the better and the wiser for the challenges, the setbacks, the twists and turns of what living a life is all about. Perfect I am not, but teachable I will always be.

Yesterday I flew across the country completing family business and returning home. Three different times I took the opportunity that presented itself to connect with "strangers," a moment of Oneness, epiphany moments that were teaching me how all the world and its humanity is our sisterhood and brotherhood . . . standing in line at the airport for screening, slow-going for the five-year-old boy and his mother in front of me . . . I commented on his "Minion" carrying case and that he must have all his most valuable possessions in it . . . then I surprised myself by saying to the mother, "I have been away from the classroom for two weeks and I miss being with kids your son's age." She replied, "I have found that all you teachers feel that way about the kids you are teaching." Oneness revealed!

Again sitting in my seat on the plane as we touched down at our destination, the lady next to me, as we rolled to our gate, began texting and calling people in her life that she had just left, telling them, "I love you, too" . . . then she began to cry softly, her feelings coming to the surface in tears dabbed away with a handkerchief amidst soft sighs of emotional release. Her husband sitting next to her patted her hand gently and caringly. We three, suspended in the confines of a small space in the plane, deep emotions and feeling of loss and separation coming, quietly almost silently flowing . . . I held my breath for a moment, not thinking about what I had left behind, but knowing that I was "at one" with the lady sitting next to me for that brief moment in time.

And lastly . . . the driver at my destination shuttling me from baggage claim to my off-airport parked car. I'm the only one in the van as he remarks, "Well, it is slow tonight and I wish I could get the rest of the night off, just spend the evening with the family. Sometimes they do that when it's slow like it is tonight." He proceeds to tell me he has a wife and four kids, one more on the way momentarily, that they live in a 27-foot RV, that he had lost a fine suburban-type home through no fault of his own, that he likes to keep busy working with his hands, and that he's going to build a cabin up in Alaska and live there with his family, growing their own food and meeting their needs by living off the land. Even with his past house misfortunes he seems philosophical, prepared to move on, surrounded by the support of his family and confident in his ability to provide a good life for himself and his loved ones. Following his bliss, I was hearing a truly unique story of a person's life . . . his dreams and its fulfillment.

This day my significant thoughts go to the powerful image and motivating force of acting and living in ways that manifest a reverence for all life. From the sacred and solemn acknowledgement of the transition of one of our brothers or sisters in Spirit to the next world, to choosing to shelter and hold in safety the most vulnerable of the animals among us, in particular our family dogs left behind when the transition of their masters occurs, the absolute dependence upon and the physical and psychological nurturing done with children who come into our lives and then pass on into their maturity and independent living, the celebration and deep spiritual bonding when we are out in nature, grateful for the inspiration and awesomeness of seasons, their changes, mountain vistas, hills, and plains, those scared places unaltered and untouched by the march and encroachment of human forces or if nature be encroached upon or impeded by humans, done gently and lovingly with minimal footprints or bending to accommodate nature and the presence of humanity in the midst of God's plentitude.

Today, I step out in trust and faith that I carry a beautiful message as a mirror being held up to each person I meet; that they/we are incomparable, unique, divinely possessed of power and purpose, self-actuated in right action, purposeful, and intentionally led into their/our greatest good . . . all totally independent and far removed from any personal thoughts of lack or limitation, self-esteem issues, or ego-induced ideas of falling short, not living up to other's expectations, or any other barriers or roadblocks that falsely have been laid in their/our path by circumstance of birth or life-generated situations. This I have come to believe for myself and so shall these other beautiful souls.

The pain is gone; the hate is no longer a living thing, only a memory of man's inhumanity to man . . . and as it recedes from our active thoughts, replaced by gratitude for and pushed out by loving thoughts of what we now have as freedom, security, and peaceful living . . . we pause, remember, and are so, so grateful for those whose shoulders we stand on.

Mother Earth, Father Sky, Sister Moon, Brother Sun: We are One in Spirit and Beingness. What affects you moves in and through me so I do not turn my back on the needs of the Earth knowing that I must not leave a footprint in the sand, but lasting thoughts only in the minds of my brothers and sisters.

In my comings and goings, I follow my instincts, my gifts, my native intelligence, my epiphany moments, my illuminations and enlightenments, yes, even my fears and foibles, into expansive experiences, into higher realms, into deeper commitments, into ever-widening connections with people, their beliefs, their humanness—ever gaining institutional knowledge and more and more embedding myself in the fabric of humanity as it shows itself to me and then passes by, offering me opportunities to jump in and be a player in the game of life.

I know I have been and continue to be that flickering candle of care and compassion to those who choose to acknowledge the Oneness between us. At the times when Spirit is felt and seen and believed to be at work in our lives, connecting in *Namaste* revelation with our larger family of brothers and sisters, woven together, inextricably and totally, we light each other's way by excellent examples of empathy and commiserating compassion, leading to reaching the highest realm of our human endeavor, our deepest humanity.

I thought the stranger was without but it was within. It is the self-same stranger that I have been carrying for these many years waiting to get out into the world, to manifest a new life, a new beginning, showing forth a God-humanitarian approach to life that betters everyone's existence. Well-being and blessings I would leave with you, though I entered unknown to you and as a stranger. I am the better for having met you and come to know you. As I reveal myself and welcome the stranger within, I make myself available to receive all who come to me as strangers but who leave as friends.

I am released, and I float above the Earth high enough to see great distances and take in a multitude of sights and scenes at a glance. The Allness of humanity spreads out before me, and I am engulfed by the epiphany moments that show me the utter unity and oneness of all creatures and creation and I am immersed in it all, separation and duality replaced by the complete knowing that Spirit and I are One and the Oneness extends to all creation.

In my current precious and invaluable moment, I get the most out of living and loving by investing myself totally and freely into my physical body and my soul-self, using but never using up the innate energy of my being to treat myself to all God's blessings, to play among God's children, both young and old, to live a life worth living and to feel, in the end, that I have left nothing undone that could have been done or not loved anyone who needed my love in that present moment.

My authentic life is one of affirming the value and uniqueness in everyone I meet; I light up a room with my enthusiasm, my gentle celebration of each person's inner beauty and Godliness, my happiness is to be in the midst of those I genuinely love and care about; I make a Divine Connection with each one's soul-self, and I leave with a grateful heart and an uplifted spirit.

I embody, embrace, emulate, and celebrate the Spirit Within Me, which prompts and prods me, caresses and cajoles me, empowers and energizes me to be peace, love, wholeness, oneness, loving-kindness, and all good things to all people.

I wait upon the promptings of the Lord for me. It comes in the ways that people hold up a mirror to my face and tell me what they see in me and who I am to them. I am so grateful! Some say I have patience, that I am a "child whisperer," that in my presence they know it's all right to be themselves, to do what they need to do, that I am a wise and compassionate listener, and one who gives wise counsel, and in all of this, am guided, guarded, and led by Spirit; to fight through the foibles and fears, the machinations, the miseries, the hurdles . . . to the hallelujahs and the celebrations of life . . . some ascending, some transitioning . . . all gloriously human, lovable, and showing up to be in my path for me to respond to. I am so blessed.

I open my heart to the realization that I can be a spiritual power-house, a divining rod for finding and exploring the loving-kindness that lies ready to serve in the hearts of my fellow-traveling spiritual beings. So many gifts of love abound among my brothers and sisters in faith, and I know that love-energy can and will be tapped and used for inspiration and deep calling, so that we can make a better world that works for all of us.

SPOUSE JOYCE IS GETTING BACK her life, after six years and more of dedicated daughter-service to her mom, who is transitioning to the serenity and calmness of an afterlife yet unknown to we the living but not to be feared, as we ply our sacred service here on Earth; as spouse Joyce has so admirably modeled for us all. We welcome Joyce back and know that Infinite Intelligence and Mind will comfort and care for her as she makes a soft landing back into her place on Earth to continue her right work.

Each person who comes into my life is a teaching moment that I shall endeavor to learn from, and I will carry some part of that person forward in my daily activities. So much outside myself has value and meaning, absorbed first by me and then carried out to expand the greater good in the world. Should my experience be celebratory or solemn, serious or frivolous, long-term meaningful or short-term enjoyable, I learn from all of it and honor each person and circumstance that helps me grow, see things differently, enrich my life, advance God's greater good in the world.

I have come to realize that every day, in every way, we are teaching each other ways of thinking, ways of going, and if we are lucky enough to cross paths with the right people, ways of serving. If we can invest our energies and our native intelligence, our intuition, dig down deep for the loving-kindness and compassion within us, we will be practicing and perfecting, honing our gifts, and honoring our path and our mission, to seek out and serve the most vulnerable, the most needy, the most deserving of our care and compassion. It is a magnificent sharing of our sacred selves, touching our humanity to that of another, acknowledging the worth and value of that person who is standing before us ... and then the words of Ernest Holmes resound more meaningfully in our hearts: "Teach and practice, practice and teach. That is all we have; that is all we are good for; that is all we ever ought to be." I am so blessed and thankful that every day, in every way I can demonstrate God in my life through sacred service to others.

Engagement in activities of the heart, involving the human condition as it is played out around us, takes work, investment of one's time, talent, and treasure, patience, taking on the ills, emotional spills, chills, and surprises that upset our well-made, well-intended but sometimes ill-advised plans, programs, dreams, and schemes for ourselves vis-a-vis others who show up in our lives. Involvement is the start when we put our toe in the water, contribute something worthwhile but intuitively knowing that we always have an out, a way to extricate ourselves from pain, remorse, reprisals, rebuffs, surprises that didn't quite fit our program.

Commitment is where we are most vulnerable, available, transparent, and willing to go the extra mile, not weighing the pros and cons of "what's in it for me." What comes back to us with commitment is the highest, deepest of human experience and engagement, a touching of soul-selves, each to each, a *Namaste* which says "I honor the place in you which is of love, light, peace, and joy. When you are in that place in you and I am in that place in me, We Are One."

The epiphany moments of our lives, when our awareness of who we are, when our deeper selves, our soul-selves are revealed in our brightest illumination of clarity, when we have at last grasped in our mind and named our specialness, our impactfulness, our usefulness to the world, comes at the very moment when our brothers and sisters in faith hold the mirror of our reality to our face and, through their actions, reactions, body language, and laudatory words of praise and celebration, show us to be more than we could ever have imagined ourselves to be. My name to others has come to be known as the "child whisperer." When it was so graciously conferred on me in a private moment with one of my colleagues, I have since carried it in me into every classroom I have visited as I put my whole soul-self out there, investing myself, embedding myself, absorbing myself into the children and their activities, and always now in some magical way making connections with someone, whereas before we were strangers, unknown to each other.

There are many places we may call home. Some of these places have come and gone, in and then out of our lives, leaving their special meaning we associate with places and experiences long gone but remembered still. Places do not stand on their own but become deeper, richer experiences when associated with people, who themselves bring perspective and a newness to those places we have inhabited. How blessed we are if we are standing, in this moment, in the sacred space of sanctuary and peace, sourcing to us the feeling of Godliness and the loving-kindness of kindred spirits, where we are knowing our usefulness, our value, where our deepest and innermost desires and needs are met, multiplied, expanded, fulfilled. Some of us have expressed to me this experience as "having been washed up on shore" as they have discovered the feeling of coming home. I am blessed for having found in my life two such places that have brought me home: Mile Hi Church and Aspen Creek Pre K-8 School.

TODAY IS A DIFFICULT DAY to wholeheartedly enter into the feeling of *Namaste* with my kindred spirits living life on this planet. Bowing to another with folded hands over my heart and thinking, "I bow to you," will be challenging for me today as I go to the County Courthouse, summoned to appear and offer myself as a juror in judgment of another's actions that may have caused harm to someone innocent of such malevolent behavior or, on the contrary, that other's actions may not have been harmful and evidence will be presented, witnesses called, facts and circumstances revealed, and justice served by a verdict of guilty or not guilty. Should I be chosen to serve in the capacity of juror, I will bring my person, my soul-self, my feelings, my emotions, and my experiences, how I look at the world as presented to me—then I will speak my truth and know that if I were on trial, I would want someone like me in the jury box to hear my case, because then I know I would get a fair and impartial hearing.

Living authentically, nonjudgmentally has its challenges when I am asked to sit on a jury deciding the fate of another human being, who either has made some bad decisions or, in part or completely, is innocent of wrongdoing. That was my challenge recently . . . to hear the facts of a criminal case, apply the laws as instructed by the judge, and render the judgment of myself and five other jurors as to the defendant's guilt or innocence, in this case dealing with five counts of alleged accused misbehavior and labeled by law to be a crime. Justice was done, we rendered a verdict, and the life of an individual was altered, perhaps forever. But in our deliberations, we jurors, in our minds, ended up somewhere balanced between punishment and rehabilitation, giving the defendant a chance to make amends, reorder their life but also to acknowledge and set things straight as to the offense. It was a great balancing act with just enough principles of humanity, compassion, love, and kindness to apply to the judicial process.

Compassion, loving-kindness, generosity of heart, empathy, consideration—are all gifts of Spirit we carry within us. How do we know to activate their power and deliver their presence into the world to be an effective change-agent for others less able to see their own inner beauty and value? How hard it is to see ourselves as carrying these gifts of Spirit, hidden perhaps deep in our soul-selves, and only subtly and quietly showing up in our daily work as we move among those we love, doing what to us may feel like the most ordinary of tasks. But our activities, to be sure, have a wider audience, greater influence, than we could ever imagine . . . It's manifestation: the planting of trees that will grow and bloom and blossom at some future time, and the shade of which we may never have the chance to sit under. Our compassion, our loving-kindness, our generosity of heart, our empathy, and our attentive consideration show up in the lives of those in whom we have invested, and our reward is knowing that we have made this world a better place than we found it.

A smile is like an open invitation from one to another to enter in and enjoy the lighter side of who I am. It is like a signal or a sign that says, in a child-like way, there is more to life than the heaviness of responsibility, of carrying the load of everyday living, of dwelling on the darker, deeper realities of life . . . so let's bag it all for the moment and just explore . . . fall down the rabbit hole and have an Alice-in-Wonderland experience together . . . the smile is the key that opens the door . . . it may even lead to peals of laughter, that is like doing mental exercises, freeing the body, being just slightly out of control, a letting go . . . . People in one of the large cities in China know the benefits of laughter being medicinal and therapeutic. Every morning in the central park of the city, they assemble just to laugh. They stand in rows, as if ready to exercise, and they just give it all up and . . . laugh, and laugh, and laugh. Then its all over and they go about their daily business. Perhaps today is the day we can set off a sequence of events where the permutations of joy are unimaginable . . . by laughing.

I love the philosophy of Science of Mind because it is really not a process that takes you ultimately to a place called "Heaven" somewhere "out there" to be experienced at some future unknown "later," but a way of living driven by the belief that we are what we think, that what we encourage to come into our minds becomes, in the long run, how we view the world, how we believe, what we become, and what we do with our life. It is a strong message that puts the burden of responsible living squarely on us, since we control our own thoughts, which lead to action or inaction, to a greater good or a complacency of complaint, excuses, self-pity, and giving up in the face of challenging conditions. When one's thoughts overwhelm any negativity, the winds of change blow insistently against one's deep-buried habits and disinclinations of resistance and in an epiphany moment, one's enlightened mind-set spills over into the outer world, seeking ways and finding means to better the lives of our brothers and sisters in our world community.

"Pray without ceasing" comes to us from the Judeo-Christian tradition, but to some of us, praying constantly, reverently, and conscientiously seems like a tall order and, frankly, not possible and still go around doing meaningful work while occupied with day-to-day living. Perhaps there is another perspective on prayer, its power, its true meaning, and how to practice it meaningfully and well. Can we see and can we say that between the time of our getting up to the time of our lying down, the time of our daily existence among our brothers and sisters in faith, that we are demonstrating prayer, that our work, our compassion, our empathy, our listening, our responding, our modeling for others a life of loving-kindness and caring attention . . . has the power of prayer, energizing and guiding us to do our right work, to be the joy and love in each other's lives? Listen to the words of Thich Nhất Hanh: "Waking up this morning, I smile. Twenty-four brand-new hours are before me. I vow to live fully in each moment, and look at all beings with eyes of compassion." *Namaste*, and have a great day.

Being quick to judge is a common trait among highly controlling, results-oriented persons moving astride through the world righting wrongs and feeling quite superior most of the time. It is a neat and orderly world of clear choices, precise analytic decisioning, condemning or espousing one viewpoint or another, feeling the rush of superiority that "it's good to be king." It tends to be a lonely world where few others are allowed in because the bar is set so high, and no mistakes are allowed.

Oh Lord, keep me humble and patient, and flying at 30,000 feet where I can see the beauty of the human landscape and not every detail of our comings and goings, each small step to be judged, codified, and summarily dismissed. May my horizons expand, my vision become crystal clear, my capacity increase for assimilating diversities of peoples, assorted thought patterns, myriad situations outside my experience, embracing all, acknowledging all, celebrating all on the altar of Oneness revealed . . . envisioning a world of love, peace, and abundance for all, serving as a spiritual beacon of personal empowerment to all.

WHAT AN ENERGIZING and powerfully compelling notion to know that my life is not broken, that there is nothing to fix, that I am enough just as I am, and that I have all the resources and means here inside me to live my best life—and the energizing power of the universe is sending me all that I need and I can use it for the betterment and beneficence of humankind.

In all this, I feel a wholeness, a Oneness, a binding congruity of purpose and intention to be the best that I can be, seeing clearly, acting with radical decisiveness, knowing success in every nook and corner, every high and low place, every shadowed or illuminated situation or circumstance, feeling healing, wholeness, and Oneness with kindred spirits, we brothers and sisters all, bound together each to each, and such binding and bonding brings out the best in ourselves, advances the highest and the most celebratory of the human condition, its finest points, its deepest compassion, as we go about doing our right work, following our brightest stars, living our best lives, in wholeness and Oneness.

I was awestruck recently when reading about Wayne Dyer's enlightened experience in realizing his calling in life was what he named "big dharma," his cosmic connection to the universe telling him why he had come into the world, a blueprint for his life's work, and his realization that all his experiences, particularly in the first decade of his life, happened to support and encourage the acting out of his big dharma, his calling, his mission in life. What a powerful, motivating force to know that what was in him and in the universe's cooperating and all-knowing guiding hand were leading him surely and certainly to follow his bliss and his reason to be. Is it not now the time for each of us to seize the moment and claim our place among the plans and the universe's expectations for our existence and our mission here on earth? Can we not see ourselves as a most magnificent part of the mosaic of life with a significant part to play in the wider world, firmly planted as spiritual beings in the midst of our brothers and sisters, all of us having a human experience, working with loving-kindness and compassion for the good of all?

I like the idea that prayer for me is not just getting down on my knees and asking for help from the One or wanting my needs and desires fulfilled, but seeing my entire life, its scope of all that I do, what I think, how I act, what moves my heart and soul, as a continuous prayer moving like a wave of compassion and loving-kindness washing over all those who inhabit, pass through, become a part of my world. When I trust that my "prayer" is working, that it is moving through the world energetically, vibrantly, powerfully, and effectively, then my expectations and enthusiasm for life are soaring and my soul-connection with my fellow human beings is felt most intensely, and I am at my happiest, most hopeful, most joyous self. I strive every day to keep this prayerful feeling of Oneness and wholeness in front of me, but as it waxes and wanes, flows or dries up, is felt or flees as an elusive shadow, I still seek out that connection to humanity and every sentient being who crosses my path and to whom I wish to have a *Namaste* experience.

There are many ways to express gratitude and gratefulness to those around us. Particularly powerful is to be generous with strangers and to act on instinct when a powerful motivation to help out, to serve another, comes over you. When 9/11 occurred so suddenly, we were all shaken with doubts and fears; the world as we had known it before was no more. My response was to look inward to my family for consoling and nurturing, and so I spent the months after 9/11 traveling across country by car every chance I could to reunite and reacquaint with family. One unexpected impact was that I became more aware and empathetic to the circumstances of strangers I met on my travels. I began leaving larger tips for waitresses at restaurants and leaving money on the table in my motel rooms for the cleaning maids to find. The tragedy of 9/11 opened my heart to be more generous not only with my money but to think again how I should be serving and relating to those around me. For me the most tragic of events opened the door of my heart to see a larger purpose in life for all of us.

Today, firmly on my path to greater glory as I fulfill my destiny, one step at a time, reaching the higher realms of my greatest yet to be, I acknowledge all who have enriched my experiences, who have modeled lives that have drawn me to them, made me want to be and do better things for this world and the beings I meet in it, who have been needy and wanting, standing before me, challenging me to go deep within myself, to discover the gifts found latently stored there, to recognize that there is a power in my word, in my personal approach to people that does indeed energize, magnetize, and coalesce all the good available in whatever situation or circumstance confronts me; I stand on the shoulders of all the sentient beings who have traveled in and out my life, whom I have called son or daughter, wife or friend, the best parts of themselves left embedded in my subconscious, to be carried by me to whatever destination needs their wisdom, their personhood, their spirit, their gifts . . . and in my taking, holding, carrying on . . . these beings remain with me on my own path to my greater good.

It was easy and comfortable in my younger years to put all others first before my own needs as it gave me purpose, a feeling of being useful and a sense of self-worth, particularly as I was raising a family, providing for their needs, and moving nicely up the corporate ladder, so I was always ready to serve the company cause in my time and energy. It was a life I felt comfortable leading and there was no concern for anything better "out there" that I might be missing. If my experiences could have been a little richer, expanded, more worldwide in scope, I did not feel the poorer for missing it. Whatever comes to me now in living a larger life of leisure and comfort, I am grateful for and am blessed to have people around me whom I care about and who in various ways, from different paths, have come into my life and enriched me. And I carry from earliest days still a life-giving fulfillment of purpose, usefulness, and self-worth as I answer the call to serve the neediest and most vulnerable among us.

Why is it easier sometimes to go out of our way, expend our energy and resources, do the right thing for someone else but when it comes to sitting back, playing the reverse role, hands outstretched, palms up, being the recipient of someone else's generosity, we deflect, turn down or minimize the generosity gratuitously given and thus in doing, we are not beholden to anyone, no favors to be returned, only perhaps a mumbled "thank you" and a swift parting out the door? To be dependent even for the smallest moment is anathema to one's general view of how one wants to be perceived . . . the fear of being looked on as not enough or as falling short. Why not allow the giving and receiving nature of the universe to play itself out in our lives through the benevolence and largesse of others? If the gift given is not usable, pass it onto someone most needy of it; if the gift be a service rendered, pay it forward, and enlarge and expand the good perceived by others to be available to all in this world we inhabit.

I AM INTRIGUED to learn more about the interplay of disease that enters a person's life, their on-going response to its progression or regression or remission, its various stages, the network of family and friends that surrounds them as a support system or the lack thereof, and how I may play a part in this human process, what that may surface in me, what skills and empathetic feelings may translate from life to a hospital setting.

Is there a void, a need to be filled, a bridge to be built across unchartered waters for me, new friends to be made, relationships to be nurtured and deepened, spiritual self to be enriched, discovered, emboldened into right action and compassionate serving of others? I see and feel now only pieces and parts, loosely joined, or ideas yet unformed, but still leading me and guiding me into right action . . . my child whisperer is speaking more loudly each day and leading me to own the "living idea" of volunteering at Children's Hospital Colorado.

In Lewis Carroll's mystical and idyllic fairy tale of *Alice in Wonderland,* Alice encounters various characters, animal, human and make-believe, who in one way or another offer her wisdom and ways of looking at things she had not thought of before. Each meeting adds insight and a new understanding for Alice as she ventures down her personal path. The Queen who believes in impossible things, sometimes thinking of six of them before breakfast, while Alice feels there is no use trying. And Alice not knowing which way to go "from here," not much caring as long as "I get somewhere," is encouraged by the Cat who says, "You're sure to get there, if you only walk long enough," . . . Are there times when "characters" have appeared in our lives to encourage, admonish, cajole, or just lift our spirits and our thoughts to higher realms of our potential and possibilities for richer living? Perhaps some offered ways of thinking and seeing things differently by their negative, dead-end behaviors or some others through modeling a way of life that resonated so positively with us that we wanted some of it. I am grateful to all who have held a mirror before me so that I could see my own perspective.

Frederick Brotherton Meyer, eighteenth-century Baptist pastor, evangelist, and Londoner by birth, once issued a stirring proclamation of right thinking when he said: "The great tragedy of life is not unanswered prayer but unoffered prayer." Turning the tables completely around and away from our own neediness, to focus on finding where the need is the greatest outside our own small sphere of wants and desires and "don't haves but must have," are there not others in more dire and doleful circumstances that need our gifts, our talents, our resources? Can we dig more deeply into the inner realm of our most heartfelt compassionate selves and find the spark of civility and radical action to make a difference in someone else's life other than our own shoring up? I have pictured in my own life of the "deus ex machina" of Greek tragedies that comes down upon Earth to save the downtrodden, and I dispensing monies as philanthropist to cure the world of its ills, but I have discovered that, though appealing, it sounded too much like "all about me." The thought occurs that my greatest gift to give is my time, which becomes more valuable as I move forward into my later hours of life.

Violence and unspeakable acts against humanity continue to plague us and challenge and shake our confidence in the future of a civilization we wish for, governed by respect for all with a foundation of Oneness and wholeness underpinning our every action. There are, however, way-showers and spiritual leaders who have appeared among us, just as in Biblical times of upheaval and human misery, to point out a better way, a way of loving-kindness and a return to love. There is a purported phenomenon observed and reported on whereby some monkeys learned to wash sweet potatoes, and gradually this new behavior spread through the younger generation until, by the hundredth monkey, this activity took a quantum leap, and all were doing it. What if this "hundredth monkey effect" were applied to the social ills of our society? If it came to pass that a significant number of human beings on our planet concentrated on, say, through meditation, prayers, issuing blessings, could we create a quantum leap, a "hundredth monkey effect," of positive change and bring such to bear on the tendencies of violence and self-destruction, leading us into higher realms of humanity valued and celebrated?

Even in the busyness of our days, in the planning and fulfilling of our daily obligations, in the acting out of the rituals and activities that make up our habitual and customary practices, is there not a small space in our hearts open to the newness of life, the welcoming in of a stranger yet unmet, the insight and intuitive knowing when to step in and be a helping hand, a nurturing heart to those in need around us? River Jordan, in her book *Praying for Strangers,* demonstrates her spiritual practice of approaching strangers every day, the ones who need a compassionate heart-connection in the moment, and says to them outright that she will be praying for them. I admire her for putting herself on the line for a stranger. For me, my years of volunteer work in schools have set up an intuitive impulse in me to be vigilant in watching for unusual and seemingly out-of-the-ordinary situations that tell me there is danger here or inappropriate activity afoot. On more than one occasion I have stepped in to question a situation, called in the proper support to settle or diffuse a potentially unsafe, harmful, or volatile situation.

The presence of hopelessness, helplessness, grinding poverty, and having slipped, little by little, or come crashing down in the tangle of unlucky circumstances is nowhere shown more clearly than on the faces of the homeless who stand at the longest traffic lights where cars are backed up; and where they can show themselves, drab and darkly sullen, and pleading with pitiful signs of scribbled words, asking for as little or as much as the more fortunate commuters can be moved to give from their hearts or instead to be hurriedly shunned away as the lowest example of how far humanity can sink. I am in my car at just such a traffic light, waiting . . . approached by one of the unfortunate ones . . . our eyes meet, his watery and bloodshot from too many days and perhaps months out in all sorts of weather, day and night . . . I am struck by our contrast . . . for today has been a particularly good day for me. I extend a gift of money to this nameless person as I ask, "Down on your luck today?" No answer, just the look I have seen before in those who are on the ropes of desperate need. In parting as the traffic light changes to green I say in a moment of compassion and enlightenment, "You know, brother, we have to take care of each other."

I believe four-square in the humanity of man, in our ability to create, expand, be more, do more, nurture with compassion, keep safe the vulnerable ones among us, persist and succeed, celebrate each other's successes, live meaningful and purposeful lives, die in the human sense with a smile and an expectation that beyond the unknown there is more to be done, vistas to climb, realms to explore, more to be, more to see, more to be a part of . . . a higher humanity, a greater usefulness, a clearer glimpse and understanding of our God, of which we are a perfect individual expression.

I learn more of my manifest destiny as I behold the multitudes of students, past and present, who march before me now, some as young men and women, others yet to be molded and to mature, and I am struck by the Oneness and unity I feel with each one of my charges entrusted to my care, and in this process I allow the divine wholeness to flow through me into ever-widening fields of human endeavor and sacred service.

Today I walk in the recognition of God's love for all, including political types who have just waged a bitter and vitriolic campaign for control of government at the highest levels of power and authority. Setting aside all animosities and anger, I see everyone coming together, each seeing with the eyes of Spirit and keeping our open hearts filled up with compassion and trust. As I walk through my world and go about doing my right work, I stand four-square for justice, social and civil, security at home and abroad, compassion across all borders, in every city, in every neighborhood, and in every hamlet and home, as I continue to follow my brightest stars, living my best life, seeking the same for all others.

CHAPTER 2

Service

The Ultimate Gift of Giving

"I slept and dreamt that life was joy.

I awoke and saw that life was service.

I acted and behold, service was joy."

— RABINDRANATH TAGORE

i n t r o d u c t i o n

s e r v i c e

Service to humanity can take many forms, serve many purposes, call for diverse skills and talents, and can be infused with high purpose and intention, synchronistic events, serendipitous moments, or just plain coincidence. My call to service ultimately has brought me into the presence of children, and within the teaching and learning dynamics of the classroom I discovered that I am more than I thought I was or could be. The school environment stimulated my desire to be useful and called upon me to use my gifts and talents for the benefit of others. It evoked in me a feeling of having come home now to a place that reflects all that I want to be and all that I need. I am blessed.

I am fortunate to have come to know more clearly my gifts and talents in this wonderful word-land of literature to revel in, to see myself as witness looking inside my creative writing process each day, enjoying those magical moments—and in the classroom to open myself up so widely, truly, and authentically to the children I have come to know and have been drawn to take a special interest in, to invest myself in their growing and learning. I am surely living my best life.

I stay strong, steadfast, visible, and eminently available to serve sacredly and consistently, diligently and deliberately, awake and aware that I am on the right path, this is the right time, and I am the right person to go about doing my right work, following my brightest stars, living my best life.

It is not "what's in your wallet," as the credit card commercial goes, but that which is in one's heart, mind, and thought—that which brings down thunder and the lightning of radical action, unselfish sacred service; it's knowing our goodness and acting on it and when I have said "yes" to it all, I open the door and answer the call.

I have many partners, both in the physical and in the spiritual realm; they lift me up so that I may see the larger me, the better life, the greater good that I have been called to deliver to the world. "I believe I can fly; I believe I can touch the sky;" they all help me to "see it, so then I can believe it." Thank you, God.

My values never waver from what they show me to be, though by false attraction or weakness of will, I reject them, temporarily traveling the slippery slope of selfish, self-centered, subtle sophistry of self-deceit; but thankfully I return to my core beliefs, a prodigal son, forever loved, always forgiven, knowing I am lifted up, dusted off, polished up, ready to serve sacredly, and grateful for the second and third chances to be useful and to be a difference-maker in others' lives.

I LIKE THE IMAGE WAYNE DYER portrayed of he and God, at the beginning of Wayne's journey in the world, discussing what Wayne was to do, what he was to become, what influences were to direct him, how he was to react to circumstances, how he was to manifest God in the world for the benefit of those who crossed his path. God reviewed how Wayne would shape and be shaped by the circumstances in his life . . . a kind of predestination, but leaving plenty of room for surprises, triumphs, heartaches . . . all the stuff humans go through on their paths.

As an older person writing this image of he and God talking, Wayne was able to look back on his past and see where he had gone this way and not that way, and where God had positioned Wayne to have the experiences he needed, to make the most of his gifts and allow he and God to work things out, all teaching moments, all for Wayne's greater good, all bringing Wayne's unique personhood to the world.

Shall we each now have a recollection of our conversation with God?

LOVING YOURSELF seems so self-indulgent and self-absorbed. Outside ourselves we are taught that the opinions and behaviors toward us are important when directed at us by people we care about and whom we want to please. The danger here is that this may require us to set aside or even reject the yearnings and desires coming from that still, small voice within that know our needs the best. We then can feel greatly misunderstood and rejected, perhaps even leading to self-doubt and confusion about our own motivations and our genuine requirements for being happy in our lives. Clarity within leads to our best possible self to serve effectively and generously the wider world around us.

Love yourself today, nurture your inner soul-self in ways that authenticate and liberate the magnificent and powerful you so that all those around you who are waiting for your self-enlightenment to emerge can benefit from your liberated spirit.

My personal call to radical right action came suddenly in an "Aha" moment from an unexpected source . . . clear, crisp, enlightened, and insistent. I was enjoying the after-dinner speakers, those who were being honored in various categories for their service to our community, an annual affair. I was basking in the reflected glory of each honored recipient, knowing that I was certainly doing my part in volunteering at schools—and doing it consistently and conscientiously for at least five years up to that time. But this one speaker, after having accepted his award with appropriate thank you's and acknowledgements to those who had helped him or influenced him . . . as a closing remark threw out a challenge to the audience, and perhaps it was not meant to be so, but it acted as a clarion call to me to expand my activities, and to do more . . . when he said simply: "If not me, then who? If not now, when?" Thank you, sir, for your wake-up call to me to make sure I am being all that I can be to make this world a better place.

Every day acts of loving-kindness and compassionate caring occur all around me if I am only awake and aware to see them. How I use their energies to breathe my own breath of love into my daily activities is the key to how successfully I am living out my life in the spirit of sacred service to humanity. Surrendering oneself and sacrificing all that does not serve, unconditional love adds spiritual energy and right action to what the world needs to see and hear from me. Every moment, every movement, every action, every reaction of mine must reflect and sound in waves of love and loving-kindness to a world in desperate need of kindly attention, spiritual modeling, right thinking, deeper awareness of the needs of others, a setting aside of personal needs and wants, and combining and coalescing one's way of going and living into the larger view of being useful and of supreme service to all who seek us—or better yet, to all whom we seek out to share our gifts.

How hard is it to receive and sustain a demeanor and consistent attitude of joy in the midst of changes taking place in our outer experiences? How do we experience the deep, relentless joy that comes when we know we are blessed and a blessing to the world? How do we show up every day with our gifts in one hand and our foibles and fears in the other? In the battle for our minds, we are shaped and fashioned by our thoughts and soon become what we are thinking. Having an existence in the world that is useful, sacred, and meaningful beyond the confines and dark catacombs of our egotistic thoughts, would be a good start, leading us to our greatest potential and opening us up to the unlimited possibilities for sacred service in this world. Feed your heart with the question "How may I serve?" and the universe will respond, "Serve with joy."

AT VARIOUS TIMES IN OUR LIFE, we pay more or less attention to our body depending on the signals, good or bad, that we receive from it, or how much we are being influenced by the messages of the popular culture that surround us day in and day out, incessant and insistent. What the influence-makers, our friends, and those we want to emulate and imitate are saying and doing is all thrown into the mix as well. How one sorts it all out and comes away with a meaningful, accurate, chance-of-success initiative and plan for self-care—one that will sustain itself through outside influences and inner body changes through time—is the key to long-term health and happiness.

When I started working out, first four times a week, then three times a week at the Rec Center I had an epiphany moment that continues to carry me forward . . . to volunteer at an elementary/middle school, to sustain it over the long haul, doing something I love . . . will take all my energy, endurance, persistence, drive, and determination, and the conditioning of my body will dictate, to a large extent, the success of my hopes and dreams on into the future.

I smile each time I recall the phrase "Leap . . . and grow your wings on the way down." It speaks to me of having courage, not because you always know what is in front of you, but because you feel a call to some sort of action. You take the risk . . . and find out later that you not only landed on your feet but that you grew in self-esteem, and the world has opened up with new experiences and companions well-met on your life's journey.

NINE YEARS AGO I entered a pre-school classroom for the first time as a volunteer, thinking this is about all I could handle in terms of what I could teach, what I had to offer. Today I am involved in the learning lives of children spanning first and second grades and on into middle school. I am teaching classes of children about the world's great books, and I am mentoring the ones who are struggling the most. This is way beyond what I envisioned for myself eight years ago. This is now my life's work, my reason to be ... I took the leap, and I have not yet landed ... I'm still soaring, following my bliss.

Dr. Kenn Gordon, metaphysical thought leader, has advanced the concept of the "living idea," an idea that resides in the Mind of God and that has inherent in it everything required to grow and to flourish ... and that does not require you, me, or anyone else to maintain it. It derives all of its requirements from First Cause, Spirit. Gordon believes huge rewards come from the practice of moving in the flow with a living idea ... matching our wants, desires, opinions, and direction with the flow of Infinite Intelligence. Having faith is the cornerstone for living in the flow.

For me, an idea emerged several years ago to offer young girls the opportunity to boost their self-image and self-esteem by offering a course at the local Rec Center focused on "exercise, movement, nutrition, stress relief, building self-esteem, and creating healthy habits that will last a lifetime," taught by Rec Center trainers and targeting middle school age girls. This "living idea" took several years before it became established, attracted resources and the attention of prime movers to move it along. But eventually, with faith in the process and staying in the flow, this course is now benefiting girls and serving as a living idea.

Even in the land of paradise surroundings, crystalline beaches, carefree thoughts far from daily obligations and commitments, Universal Law is at work creating synchronicities and opportunities to view a larger horizon, a longer view, a higher realm of needs to be addressed, to be filled ... gifts of self to be given. Two days before I leave on vacation, feeling glad to move away from my school volunteer service, I see a local newspaper article of a young lady working with a Children's Hospital volunteer staff to bring stuffed animals to the children confined to hospital beds. The article sticks with me.

I get to my vacation spot, start enjoying the beach surroundings, unwinding, taking in the diverse and relaxing environment . . . when suddenly an idea serendipitously comes to me . . . volunteer at the Children's Hospital for the summer. I had no intention prior to this time . . . in fact I worked not to have my time taken up tutoring, etc., and here I am filling out an online application to volunteer . . . The universe opened the door to yet another opportunity to serve, and I am answering the call.

CHAPTER 3

Family & Legacy

The Imprint of Our Lives

"The true meaning of life is to plant trees,

under whose shade you do not expect to sit."

— NELSON HENDERSON

i n t r o d u c t i o n

f a m i l y & l e g a c y

In my journey of self-discovery, I have come to appreciate the concept of family in the broadest of meanings and its impact on individuals as a nurturing force to live by, to sacrifice for, to protect, to teach, and to learn from. Inclusive words for family might be: immediate, extended, school, work, church, military, neighborhood, society; each having its own outward folkways and mores, its own behavioral code of conduct and expectations, with an underlying common bond to, above all, sustain human existence.

We are born into lineage not of our own choosing but gratefully receiving the joy of life and identity, thereby to, then, in our own unique lifetime of being and becoming, create a legacy to pass on to future generations. If we could convince ourselves that it is not presumptuous to believe that we are immortal, what inspirational avenues of endeavor would open up to us and shout loudly and clearly, "Legacy!"? What elements of ourselves would we like to see remain after we have transitioned, that speak most clearly of who we were and how we would most want to continue to be reflected in the world that we have left behind?

*H*ere is an everyday miracle: to first imagine and then realize that our family owns a lake cabin above the shores of Lake Columbine in sight of the Never Summer Intermountain Range, a landmark and figurehead of prominence featured in the Rocky Mountain National Park.

Snowmobiles are king here in this snowmobile capital of the world or at least in Colorado, as the local chamber of commerce reminds us. Picture our family's first Christmas spent in this Winter Wonderland and on cue Christmas morning, it starts to snow and lasts all day through present openings, festive meals, loud play, and laughter and into the evening. I look out each window from time to time at the scene as if to remind myself that I am really here and this is all for real, a dream the family has had, now come to fruition. For me, my only experience growing up in Chicago with such as this is when I would shake a snow globe as a child and dream of being in the midst of swirling snow and caroling choruses.

I carry the Divine within me today as I navigate and maneuver through the halls of airports, parking lots, good-byes and hellos of family, and reflections of times past and things to come. In the turmoil and tremors of emotional ups and downs, I pray that the Divine within keeps me in gratitude for my living this moment, this day, this life.

With all the deep distractions and threats to life as we know it going on around family and around the world, we raise our spirits and our minds to that Intelligent Being who sees all, knows all, and is everything worthwhile and of the highest good in ourselves and in the world around us. Gratefully and humbly I am thankful for being put in this place, at this time, with family, to reflect and celebrate the Goodness of God.

I RECALL NOW how, as a child, I took life quite seriously. Even my play seemed to always have a purpose, an escape from what I perceived but early on could not name as my parents' hard life of providing for five children. Their troubles persisted day after day, unrelenting, but they used their energies to shield us children from the realities that life— a struggle that required constant hard work and diligent practice and fortitude to make a go of it. My parents found ways to enjoy life amidst struggle and life's daily pressures, among their many friends and family, but it was a boisterous and hard-living lot of companions who, for the most part, laughed loud and enjoyed life.

My inner life called me to a gentler, more introspective demeanor among the family frivolities, keeping myself mindful of work to be done, making contributions of money to the family as I got older and found meaningful paying jobs as a teenager living at home. Through this process I developed and constructed a life of useful work as my mantra, a desire not to ever be a burden, and a feeling of ultimate accomplishment when I could be of service to those around me.

Today my thoughts go back to the image and person who I was privileged to call Mom. She was elegant and gracious in her demeanor and disposition. I do not recall a word of anger ever coming from her lips. She created an atmosphere of love and security around me from which I could always find a safe harbor of receptivity and nonjudgment in which to thrive. In her eyes, she reflected back to me that I could do no wrong, and every day of my life I strove to prove my worth as she saw me. Always gentle of spirit, shy and yet strong, always working behind the busy stage of raising five children, watching pennies to make ends meet, always looking beautiful and statuesque wherever she went. My Dad's breath she must have taken away when they first met and fell in love. Her birthday was on the Fourth of July and for many years, growing up, she thought that the fireworks were just for her, celebrating her birthday. My greatest tribute to her is that I felt a special kindred spirit that we shared together, and that who I am today inwardly mirrors much of what she was in the world.

TODAY I AM GRATEFUL for the insight to know and to celebrate each level of fatherhood that has come into my life as teacher and as companion on my path. I honor my Earthly father as a worker and family provider who taught me the meaning of responsibility, the value and worth of hard work for others, and instilled in me the desire to always be useful in the service of others. To my Earthly father, I wish now to offer closure and peace through mutual forgiveness and reconciliation. I honor my Heavenly Father and pray that I be open to receive His grace, to rediscover and honor His presence and to allow Him to save my soul.

I honor my sons as fathers for reminding me of life cycles, the precious passage of time to be fully aware of and to enjoy, and the pride I feel as I hand them the scepter of fatherhood. I honor the grandfather I have become, the length and breadth, which has meant so much to me and stretched me beyond family to others in need of a grandfather, my learning new ways to give and receive love and to share joy in a special way. I honor all other fathers who have made contributions to my personal development, growth, and maturity as a parent and who have taken an interest in my own children and grandchildren.

Today, the Fourth of July, is the date of my mother's birth. The day after Christmas several years earlier was my father's birthday. Later I learned that my mother-in-law was born on Christmas Day, some ten years after my parents were born. One ongoing reaction my mother had until she knew better was that all the fireworks going on as she celebrated her birthday were in her honor. She was such a great lady and a perfect mom for me. I wish I had thought of giving her a special salute of fireworks on her birthday. I don't know about my mother-in-law and my dad, but it must have been a bummer year after year to be overshadowed and overwhelmed by the Christmas festivities, even though everyone tried hard to make them feel special on their birthdays.

Birthdays can affect different people in different ways. A boy in first grade where I volunteered cried every time we celebrated one of his classmate's birthdays because he wanted it to be for him. With twenty-five students in the class, he cried quite a lot that year and may still be crying yet. Oh, the foibles and fortunes of birthdays.

THERE IS NO OTHER EXPERIENCE like watching Chicago Cubs baseball at "The Friendly Confines," Wrigley Field. I know exactly where
I sat with my dad for many games, circa 1948 when I was ten years old.
They were the "lovable losers" then but the Cubbie faithful cheered
them on as if they were the World Champs. We would sit out beyond
the third baseline near the ivy-covered outfield walls in left field where
you could almost touch the likes of Cub favorite Andy Pafko, "Old
Peruska," fondly nicknamed, and later Hammerin' Hank Sauer, sure
to please the crowd when he'd hit a home run on to Waveland Avenue.
Now the Cubs are standing tall, best record in the league and about to
go deep into the postseason, not a doormat of the league anymore.
Electronic scoreboards have replaced the need to have pencil and score-
card ready as the line-ups were announced over the PA system by Pat
Piper. As the saying goes, "This is not your father's team," with the
passage of time, names and faces have changed, but thanks, Dad, for
the memories of summer afternoons with you at the ol' ballpark.

CHAPTER 4

Spirituality

Manifesting the Divine Within Me

"We believe that the Universal Spirit, which is God, operates through a Universal Mind, which is the Law of God; and that we are surrounded by this Creative Mind which receives the direct impress of our thought and acts upon it."

— ERNEST HOLMES

i n t r o d u c t i o n

s p i r t u a l i t y

I cannot hold back, stand out of the way, look from afar, take the low road, stay out of the fray, in safety, contentment, and self-satisfaction, unmoved and untouched by the needs and wants of humanity crying out for retribution and surcease, just out of my reach but within sight and hearing. I must be courageously engaged and put myself in the middle of that which calls to be discovered, uncovered, made known, shown, taught, learned, pulled out of imagination and creative idea into manifested form and substance; and its right standard and test must be that it serves the greatest good for all — and I pledge myself to be at the forefront of its happening, knowing that I am guided by Spirit and Divine Intelligence.

I open my heart and my soul-self to receive promptings and urgings from Divine Mind, to harmonize and unite my physical world with my spiritual inner workings of Spirit.

This means staying aligned and balanced in my world with thoughts and ideas creatively congruent with Divine Mind so that the Divine Plan for my life may flow authentically, smoothly, usefully, and expansively into my greatest-yet-to-be. I have only to put myself in an attitude of receptive belief and trust and my expanded consciousness will accept the truth, absorb its message, and reflect it out into the world.

I rely on the Christ mind to move me forward, to enlighten my understanding, to halt and fill in the cracks and crevices of my consciousness yet in the shadows of doubt and dubious thinking, held back and hindered at times from my seeing beyond the yet unknown, the things that go bump in the night, that which threatens to impede, diminish, destroy, turn aside, devalue what the Christ mind holds up and knows is life-giving, expansive, a pearl of great price, everlasting bliss and beauty . . . and so I let go of all thoughts of lack or limitation, short-sighted scenarios of limited seeing or believing. I am now firmly entrenched in the comfort and confidence of the Christ mind, the All-Pervasive Intelligence, the Omnipresent Omniscient One that guides and guards me on my path, progressing ever upwards and onward, as I run the race of life to the finish line that in reality never ends but always holds out more, deeper, higher, further of all that is good and very good.

Nothing shall claim me but the love of Christ I send out to the world; it replaces, supplants, sends away, dismisses any and all fearful images, thoughts, or demonic shadows, then deposed of and delivered far beyond any influence or inflammatory effect on my life.

My "bigger" self has many parts and pieces, some Earth-bound mortals like myself and some soaring spirits that urge me on to my greatest good; the "outer" is my "vehicle," my demonstration, to know that my "inner" God-self is moving and having its way with me in all that I do and say.

My God is the Potter, and I am the clay; "It is not my will, but thine be done, Lord." This is the mindset that activates and energizes within me the power of God and my potential to turn loose and unleash the unlimited possibilities in myself and show others that which they may not think they are capable of doing. Within my surrender are the seeds of the greatest good ready to be planted, cultivated, watered, grown, and harvested in mine and the hearts of my brothers and sisters in Christ, Our God. Surrender is victory, letting go is receiving abundantly, jumping into the unknown is sprouting wings to fly, giving everything away is receiving all in return. Sitting in the lowest place, you will be called to sit in the place of honor at God's table.

"LET GO AND LET GOD" is a powerful mantra for effective living in today's world. We are invited constantly from the "talking heads" in the media to be swayed or disswayed by their opinions and their so-called expertise. We are pushed and pulled, persuaded and dissuaded, cajoled and embarrassed, pleaded with, shown the absolute authenticity of arguments for or against, products to use, actions to take, which if not used or taken may result in dire consequences or missed opportunities.

So we must ward off and avoid cluttered thinking and powerfully motivated distractions and downright dangers to our soul, our integrity, our self-worth . . . and continually remind ourselves that we are made of God, that we have the Mind of God, that it is ours and we can use it . . . and that following Divine Direction, soaring above the trappings and pitfalls of our mundane, soulless cultural inclinations, we make a real impact in the world, leave a legacy of love for future generations to emulate.

The Father and I are One; I am in Him and He is in me; corporally and mystically we are bound each to each; He speaks through my worthiness to demonstrate His Presence and His Purpose. If not me, then who? If not now, when?

The God you are to me is the Divine Within Me, not a god outside, separate and apart. You have invited me into your Oneness, and I accept through my thoughts and my radical action to demonstrate "Spirit is with me."

The Spirit of the Divine Within Me manifests and demonstrates, acts and speaks, transforms and expands within the confines and the boundaries of our physical world, wherein peace, love, and harmony powerfully prevail over evil and violence, and I know I am a part of this process of givingness and loving-kindness.

I have felt the Divine Within Me before, speaking to me sometimes lucidly, sometimes as looking at myself through a mirror darkly. Today I can name my clarity, my vision, my epiphany moments as a touchstone of great price, to trust when It appears, and to act with radical action when It calls me to do so.

I run the race I have never run before; I walk through doors that I always ignored before; I believe what my intuitive self is saying and where I am being led: I see the goodness in my life and ignore what appears to be shortcomings and deficiencies in my person; I am alive and well and living the life of Godliness and Christ-centeredness.

I am Grace-filled, Grace-directed, Grace-commanded—to be, to experience, to reach, and to expand into my greatest yet-to-be in communion and Divine inspiration with other sentient beings along my path.

I live, breathe, and have my knowing in the absolute certainty that there is a universe of enough and I am in it. Spirit resides, abides, and provides within its dimensions for my needs and wants, and I live in joyous anticipation of its magnificent magnitude and multiplicity of abundance.

I washed up on the shore of Mile Hi Church, a place where gratitude, new spiritual beginnings, forgiveness, community, the feeling of "I have arrived and I am now home and at peace" prevail—all come together, stranded no more, sure and assured with God's embrace, nurtured by those around me and in this environment of abundant love.

I know that the inner must be made known in the outer if ever I am to achieve and contribute to creating the greatest good of God among peoples. To do this is my sacred calling.

I look around me, and I am so grateful for all the visible signs of God holding me in safety and the assurance of abundance everywhere apparent in my life.

I turn on my Higher Power knowing it works for me in everyplace I go, with everyone I meet, in every situation that greets me, in every need that seeks me to address it.

I go forth not alone but having the Divine Within, guiding, guarding, gratifying, giving greatness, greeting all who come into my field of activity of loving-kindness.

The inner directs the outer should I allow it; the spiritual speaks to the temporal should I trust it; the voice within decides and guides the power of my word, which goes out and does not come back to me void. My thinking prepares for the unconditional presence of Spirit to reside and abide and set aside all distractions so that I may commune with my soul-self, unfettered by the clutter and clamoring of disjointed, dissident murmurings of lack and limitation.

God is everywhere; God is inside me; God gives me everything I need. Thank you, God.

I pierce the veil of deceptive and desultory appearances in this "world of 10,000 things" (as described by Lao Tzu), to find the esoteric, the immutable, the undefinable, the Uncaused Causation, the Alpha and the Omega of all animate and inanimate creations—and when I am in the center of all of it, I greet my soul-self, and I am home.

I invoke the Spirit of my being to guide me through the ebbs and flows of my human experience and as a "rolling stone gathers no moss," I take away from each encounter, from each experience, that which will serve me best in the Game of Life, and I bless and thank all that has served its purpose up to now, contributors all to my greater-yet-to-be.

I know that joy walks with me at every step, though sometimes cloaked and clouded . . . hidden by physical circumstances that challenge us with judgment, personal pain, opinions of others, our own inadequacies and foibles . . . joy offering itself as a Divine alternative to the miseries of this world. Joy takes us out of our ego-hurt and moves us to higher realms, tapping and touching our spiritual soul-selves, which cannot be diminished or defeated by the darker aspects of humanity.... So we stand as one, welcoming joy, newly found and clothed in perfect timing for our needs, to nurture and celebrate our humanity and our spirituality.

If I first believe it, then I will see it; and fear and trepidation will recede from the places I go when confronted with obstacles and tight places in my living. Circumstances and situations may not be alterable but my thoughts about them are in my control, for sure. I am powerful when I believe and then see that God is with me in all things and in all ways, no matter what, no matter where.

"THERE IS A POWER WITHIN ME, and I can use it." So says the wayshower Ernest Holmes, encouraging us to look inside ourselves, acknowledge our strength within, push it to the surface of recognition, affirm its power and potential in our lives, nurture its possibilities, dream its reality into existence, raise it up, celebrate it, sing gratitude for it, and then go into the world and demonstrate its eternal and infinite existence with our mind to the Mind of God. "One must bring one's self to the place in mind where there is no misfortune, no calamity, no accident, no trouble, no confusion, where there is nothing but plenty, peace, power, life, and Truth" (Ernest Holmes, *The Science of Mind*, p. 295).

It is immensely empowering to know that whenever I think, I am using the Mind of God. Even in times when my thoughts and actions challenge my integrity and my self-esteem by reflecting a person that is not who I am or want to be, I still am firmly placed in the hand of God, leading me, teaching me, taking me toward a better place. Eventually the way is illuminated, my soul-self delivers the messages that raise my value in my own eyes, puts me in balance, sets me right, and takes me home. And I embrace the knowing that I have lived a life worthy of having been lived because all the dark nights of my soul have been replaced by God's illumined presence, every step of the way.

That which comes to us cloaked in the dark shadows of uncertainty or remorse or self-doubt is not to be viewed as our being thrown down the stairs into the dark night of the soul. We have put ourselves there with the cluttered thinking of our monkey minds that, in the first instance of our despair and deeply dark thoughts and jumbled-up judgments, makes us out to be the villains and bad people in a version of the story of our life we would have wished to forget and to certainly have avoided. But all that is wishful thinking.

It's here now, squarely in front of us, a done deal. . . . How now do we respond? How about asking from the heart, "What is the good I am not seeing yet?" Using our mind and the Mind of God we can deconstruct and let go of the stuff that keeps us rigidly and catatonically in the dark thoughts of our own choosing, and lift ourselves up into the light and love of the Divine where Spirit can work with us through to our greatest good.

I love the simple but powerful truth taught in the Science of Mind philosophy that everything you need to know to live the life of your dreams is already inside of you. It takes all the pain and struggle out of searching and seeking approval, affirmation or forgiveness from any outside source for having done or failed to do some standard of behavior or excellence imposed by the external world. This does not mean running amok or wanton behavior is condoned or encouraged. It clarifies our destiny, our bliss, our responsibility to be awake and aware, to model to the world a God-directed loving-kindness, and to answer the clarion call of sacred service wherever the Spirit within leads you. It takes you deeper into self-discernment, urging you on to find your gifts, to celebrate them, to follow you bliss. Dwell within, be generous with your self-praise, and know in your heart of hearts that everything you need to know has already been given to you. Just knock, and the door shall be open to you.

GRACE IS ONE INFUSION into the creative process that adds depth and meaning to what comes out as a "living idea." Grace has the tinge of spirituality, the essence of divine purpose, the power and strength of living, and the longevity to sustain itself through crisis, doubt, criticism, and apparent failure. But deep down if there is a grace-infused power of intention, a chance to affect profound change in one life, in this moment, able to ripple out in gentle waves of influence for a higher purpose, a greater good, a worthwhile change to the human condition of one person, one family, one community . . . then authentic grace is surely operating in the midst of the manifestation unfolding . . . the "living idea" is born, is nurtured, is powerfully speaking the truth, and the grace of that truth is infusing the collective creative process that will surely lead us home.

On my journey through life, particularly in more recent days, I have begun to see the value of being more patient and letting life come to me, allowing things to show up in their own good time, not putting a fence around what I need and want to happen, not constructing a safe and predictable future while I'm standing still in the present. Boxing myself in does not allow the Universe to act powerfully and effectively in my life when I am making all the rules and creating a predictable, uninspiring "World According To Roger." Not all that exciting!

We are a part of the Mind of God. Our mind can make this Divine Connection, and we can use its power for our living large in this world. Be still and know that you are eminently and magnificently successful. Know that you are abundantly provided for through your own initiative, divinely inspired. Know that your perfect health supports and sustains the energies you pour into your work of sacred service. Know that you are the love of God touching lives in your world simply because you know who you are and who you are becoming.

It is hard to look at yourself in the mirror and proclaim in each and every instance, circumstance, and situation, day in and day out, through thick and thin, buffeted by the winds of chance and change . . . that you are awesome and magnificently constructed of the stuff that Divine Substance is made of . . . but if you believe it, you will see it. The universe stands ready to respond with divine intelligence to that which you believe yourself to be. This is no ego trip but God calling for your soul-self to be awakened to the power of your presence in the world. Each day there is work to be done, miracles to witness and be a part of . . . no time to start way back in the dreariness of past "shoulda's, woulda's, and coulda's," because your awesomeness and your magnificent soul-self longs to be revealed and turned loose in the world so others may plug into its power and its light, into its potential and its promise, into its awesome reality and right action.

How comfortable are we with being alone in the stillness and silence of our soul-selves, seeking nothing, wanting nothing . . . just listening, opening to what is around us, slipping quietly into its oneness, surrendering to its allness, feeling the omnipresence of Spirit taking us over? Where would such an experience likely happen for us? Does it need to be in a place uncrowded with people, away from the insistence of the everpresent iPhone, out in nature . . . at our favorite thinking place . . . desert, mountains, ocean . . . wherever peace and tranquility overcome time and the temptation to be doing? Can we close our eyes, open them again, realizing time has passed, not knowing where we have gone to for the moment, but knowing it has been a pleasant, dream-like experience, knowing that Spirit has just visited us, has left a subliminal, subtle message that will seek us out later to be used and useful in extraordinary and wonderful ways? Is this not a so worthwhile thing to look forward to . . . a meeting with God?

ONE OF THE MOST FREEING MOMENTS one can have is to come to the realization that the true God is the personal God within and not some external God, the image of a judging, watching authority figure, keeping all things in order through a stern, overseeing visage meant to be sure that It and Its laws are obeyed. This is what many of us might have called The Church of Our Youth, when as youngsters growing up, adult authority was all that we knew, and that was carried right into the churches we attended. That was then; it served us in various ways— security, certainty, a place to make amends if one had "sinned"—but now embracing a deeply personal God-relationship within, we enter partnership with the Divine, a powerful one-on-one connecting soul-force, where our dreams, desires, our destiny is linked inextricably with God's will for us, where we seek and find clarity, vision, peace, love, abundance for our lives and where what we seek is conjoined with God's will to provide us. And we carry this powerful connected spiritual source with us as we go through the day doing our right work.

I love the divine idea that there is God within us speaking quietly and calmly, directing our soul-self into higher realms of realization, empowerment, and deeper intuitive knowing . . . and its reality touches us on every side through nature and our connection to all of humanity. For some it may arrive like an "Aha" moment, an inner physical chill of recognition, an intuitive feeling of directionality, an inner symbol calling for deeper contemplation, observation, silence, listening. I visualize myself on some paramount vista, a mountaintop, quietly surveying the scene, empty of busy thoughts, a vessel to be filled, and, using the image given to us by our Native brethren, I see a wisp of smoke messaging to me and I hear the muffled and murmuring staccato beat of the moccasin telegraph pounding and sounding insistent on my consciousness, and I listen, I interpret, I proceed with courage and confidence into my future . . . following my bliss, expanding into my greater-yet-to-be.

Is it true that you can make God laugh just by telling Him your plans? And why would this be so? Perhaps we come to realize that no matter how tightly we bundle the details of every step in our planning process and how attached we become to the outcome, fate, circumstances, unforeseen serendipitous scenarios rise up to crush our contentment—or surprise of all surprises—to give us something better than what we had wished for. Our ideas were neatly packaged in a box, tied with a ribbon . . . ready to be experienced, but the universe had other places for us to go and people to meet.

Being attached to outcome is having weights attached to your body while you're trying to run the Race of Life. Surrendering to what is in front of your face can be liberating, with high reward payoffs in pleasant surprises and enriched experiences. Ramana Maharshi reminds us, "Let come what comes, let go what goes. See what remains." And what remains is perfect for your authentic self to work with, to benefit others you meet on your path, and to provide you with an enriching, soul-satisfying life.

I feel empowered knowing that I am worthy of every blessing and good fortune, unlimited abundance, all the fruits of life, limitless opportunities to grow, prosper, and give some really magnificent gifts to the world. I am geared up for radical right action, enthused, inspired, energized, all of this . . . to contribute whatever is in me to the betterment of humankind, one soul at a time.

And the beauty of it is that the universe stands ready to work with the Spirit within me to achieve, accomplish, celebrate, and demonstrate myself as a worthy servant leader, imbued with the fire and fortitude of giving useful sacred service to all who cross my path. There is a guiding light of spiritual significance, universe-directed and God-inspired, which has guided me on my path, showing me where and how to unfold and display my gifts to the world, nudging and urging me into deeper waters of personal expansion and allowing me to express my inner soul-self on a road of self-discovery and self- illumination. . . . I know I am worthy of all of it.

THE PRACTICES OF DECLARATION AND AFFIRMATION are powerful tools taught in the sanctuaries and school rooms of the practitioners and advocates of the Science of Mind philosophy. They are spoken with the authority of Universal Law, complete conviction, absolute certainty, without reservation, with a knowing that goes beyond any secular definition or worldly understanding. They need no proof or assurance of outcome, just complete and steadfast faith that if one believes and thinks upon a certain outcome without putting a picture of what it must look like or any sort of visualization to prove it has occurred, forces and energies of universal magnitude and magnificence are set free to create all circumstances and situations to meet the essence of the declared and affirmed desire.

As I stand on the threshold of new beginnings I worry not whether to go this way or that, start this or end that, think one way and not another, work hard in this direction, ease off in the other. It will all come to me in its good time. And when I get a "living idea," in Dr. Kenn Gordon's parlance, I shall know it, throw my energies into it, and not be concerned about the size nor shape of outcome.

I believe there is no God other than the Universal Divine Intelligence that resides within each of us, standing ready to put into reality that which our thoughts, beliefs, perceptions, and views of the world around us have created. There is no benign fatherly God outside ourselves meting out rewards and punishments to Its children, according to their behaviors. It is what is inside of us, our soul-selves, our conscious, living, breathing, perceiving self that guides us down our path. What we believe is what we see. What we perceive is what we receive.

So it is upon us to "cast our nets" in such a way that our mindset, our thoughts, our beliefs . . . lead us into higher realms of right action, grace-filled living, joy, peace starting within and then bursting forth to co-create with Universal Intelligence that which we have perceived and desired in our lives. Whatever we wish for or dwell on in mind is acted on by Divine Intelligence to give us what we believe; so it is our choice, our power to live bountifully and free or shackled by the shadows of lack and limitation. The Universe stands ready to serve.

CHAPTER 5

Personal

Insights and Illuminations of Inner Wisdom

"Hindsight — *Wisdom Gleaned From Past Experiences*
Insight — *Knowledge Gained In the Present Moment*
Foresight — *Believing and Becoming*"

— ROGER T. BERG

"The more you see yourself as what you'd like to become, and act as if what you want is already there, the more you'll activate those dormant forces that will collaborate to transform your dream into your reality."

— WAYNE DYER

introduction

personal

I know I am on a path of self-discovery. There have been signs and signals, illuminations, enlightenments, and epiphany moments that have informed me, roads taken and roads not taken, things I have learned and what I have yet to discover about myself in the wider world. May I share with you some of these moments that have made up my journey thus far?

I bring my most active thoughts to life as I ponder them, the feelings they generate, and the insights they bring as I copy kinesthetically the Science of Mind *magazine's Daily Guides and follow its discussion. I rerun in my mind my actions and reactions to persons and events, allowing unresolved issues and sticking points to be replayed in an atmosphere of empathy and compassionate interaction.*

Surfacing in this process of illumination and self-talk are the current state and strength of my traits, beliefs, goals, accomplishments, and the lessons currently being taught to me. Whatever in terms of residual or direct sadness, anger, hurts, and fears are surfacing, I allow them to show themselves in this quietude and serene place of heart at this moment. Enlightenment and epiphany moments bring clarity, direction, peace, and renewed intent and resolve to go on.

I write and ponder the current state of my life, my affairs, my right work, my brightest stars, and above all, a supremely assured knowing that I am being led by Divine Intelligence and Spirit that wishes to use me for purposeful and useful work, before any inevitable end comes to this chapter of my best life.

Should God grant me the grace of illumination to see my legacy even as I am in the midst of its unfoldment, I wish for it to be the image of softer days, full of celebration and praise, alive with useful pursuits, praise, permeated with the laughter of little children, halos of hope wound around their heads, nothing to fear, safety always near, love and respect abiding and abounding . . . and years later when the sharp, clear images of each moment having fled from memory, may there be an after-glow of gentle remembrance that still has the pure power of intention, purpose, and meaning to, even then, be useful to humanity.

I resolve to declutter every floor and room in the apartment house of my mind, sweep it all clean, rearrange the furniture of my thoughts, the focus and direction of my vision, dreams, and hopes, bring in, exam, revise, energize, prioritize, and imbue with high intention and purpose a spiritual blueprint and path to use my gifts, seek out and find new resources, refashion and rejuvenate what skills have come along with me, let go of what is no longer useful, step out in faith, have patience, and blend in with the life plans and necessary arrangements that make life work for others, be a cooperative spirit and facilitating influence to all whom I meet, and begin anew with an apartment house of mind ready to meet the future, ready to expand God's greatest good and loving-kindness across all cultures, in all situations and circumstances, for all time into eternity, a living legacy.

I wish to remove all barriers in my seeking and finding where my good lies. There is a treasure trove of experience passing through my life which, if I be awake and aware, provides me with attractive opportunities to examine, accept, or reject, and in so doing in the process, expand, be enlightened, see things differently, provide support, feel more deeply, be in touch more with my humanness, climb to a higher realm of com-panionship and sense of community, be completely wrapped up and nurtured in my greatest good, my spiritual soul-self, the furthest reach and power toward my self-actualization and my greatest yet-to-be.

I am an "institutional" person, comfortable in the larger sense of community, in well-established patterns of behavior and ways of doing and coming and going. . . . A loyalty to a bigger entity, a greater essence, a higher truth, a deeper meaning is in me.

"I believe I can fly; I believe I can touch the sky" (R. Kelly). . . . I open the door in what I believe is a three-room house and on the other side it opens up to reveal my house is really a mansion; I just didn't know it.

I make my plan; I leave room for surprises and moments of teaching and learning; I take my hand off the wheel and try to not control interpretations or outcomes; I set my sails, sit in the back of the boat, and allow myself to go onshore in distant lands, anticipating no end point but as witness, enjoying the process.

My within seeks to get without; my deepest dreams deserve expression, and so I wait, wanting, willing, wishfully; but I hide inside and chide myself; patience and peace, please come.

I know that the Divine is within me; that it manifests and demonstrates loving-kindness and the Greatest Good through my good works and sacred service; that I am projecting God's Goodness into everyone I come in contact with; I am a living luminary of loving light available for all to plug into as they become enlightened and energized for their greater good.

I come from a place of deep and abiding connection through the music and lyrics of certain songs that connect to my feelings and emotions at one point in time . . . then it dissipates, leaving me melancholic or euphoric as the case may be . . . At least I know that I am alive.

Now, this moment in time, is all I have to instruct me, to teach me, to show me the illumined path to my greatest good. The past is gone; the future is not yet come; the present opens my awareness to unlimited opportunities and incredible experiences for ways to make a difference in my world of now and forever now.

I climb and I reach higher realms, the higher ground of experience and challenges, going through storms and wild weather; through wilderness and wonderment, seeking silence and serenity; finding only, at first, trials of troublesome turmoil and distrust. Confidence builds, momentum builds, belief in God and oneself gets the upper hand; I move higher, ground is gained and retaken; the view from the top tantalizes and treats me to the ecstasy of existence.

The tapestry of my life is like a coat of many colors, hues, and blendings. The pattern is sometimes beautifully coherent and clear in direction, whereas other parts show a meandering design, a darkly hidden meaning, one of harder deciphering; but stepping back, I can see clearly, coming out into the light of epiphany moments, a redirection to higher realms, to God-like living, escaping dark nights of the soul, celebrating moments along a better path, a brighter tomorrow, a triumphant today.

MY CURRENT SOLITARY EXISTENCE while my spouse is away on family business has left me with impressions and insights into my life that are highly impactful for my going forward, namely I lose my egocentric self, my concern for what is going to happen to me, the fear that life is shortening for me. Have I done enough, or have I done too much squandering of time?

When I am in the presence of children, I get lost in them, in their beautiful soul-selves, in their vulnerabilities, in their shameless and spontaneous displays of emotion . . . both pleasure and pain . . . the awesome responsibility I feel to their dependence on me to show them a world according to Mr. Roger, one that takes them to a different place than they have been before, show them what they know, only in a new magical creative light, makes them delighted with being alive, at that moment, makes them happy to be who they are, and to go away from our encounter wanting to feel that way again.

This is what I wish to seek and repeat in the New Year, and so I have exciting work to do . . . to make myself vulnerable, available, skillful, authentic, celebratory, whimsical, tough-loving, compassionate, optimistic, grateful—and I am so thankful and so eager for these kiddos to show me how to live an authentic life.

Most assuredly, I have come to know that looking at things differently, asking more questions than purporting to know all the answers, being more patient . . . less judgmental, choosing humility . . . letting go of arrogance, loving the moment, living large, seeing the inner beauty of every man, woman, and child I meet on my path . . . giving, receiving from each our special treasures and gifts . . . all of this new and expanded perspective brings love and light into my life where there had been heavy responsibility, falling short, feeling inadequate, undervaluing myself.

When life seems "like a box of chocolates" and you don't know which one to pick to get the most out of the experience, be guided by the thought that what is underneath each sample, unseen and unknown, is all good because they all are held together in the wonderful Oneness of chocolate, which is clearly known and loved by you. You can't go wrong, and remember, there are no coincidences, only synchronistic happenings, so choose which chocolate to take . . . it's not random. . . . You are guided—and it's all good!

Sometimes I am sorrowful and doleful to see beautiful and blissful events like sunrises, sunsets, and weeks at my favorite beach locale come and so quickly go, either by its own leaving or by my needing to give it up because it's time to pack up and go home. It almost feels like a risk not to be taken, an investment in it not to be made, because in the end it will all be taken away and nothing will remain but a distant memory. But perhaps that is the purpose and the lasting impact on us . . . to create and hold the memories we have constructed out of our moments, our days, our lifetime. In the present moment, we can make our memories what we want them to be for us today . . . that will be their reality, and they will come alive through our imagining them, reliving them, reviving them, honoring them, and celebrating them in our hearts today.

To remain calm, cool, and collected in the midst of adverse conditions swirling around me is a great skill that I am yet learning on a daily basis in my life. To listen patiently and allow those around me to take courses of action, to make decisions, to choose or not choose one direction to go or not to go . . . when I have definite opinions about the matter, judgments about the person or situation, my own personal prejudices, predispositions and disinclinations, ego-chatter in my head trying to tip me one way or another, monkey-mind, not enough sleep, whatever . . . to go deep into the safety and security of the stillness of my "thinking place" brings perspective and summons great power and perspicacity to any situation. Here, I am speaking of circumstances I come across on a daily basis in the classroom or discussing life choices with family members who may be at the crossroads of choosing direction and emphasis in their lives.

IN MY CURRENT LIFE OF WANDERING, wondering, and discovering new ways of thinking and looking at events showing up in my life, a recurring and powerful theme acting itself out in front of me is that there are no coincidences, and serendipitous moments are happening to and around me all the time, if I only pay attention to them. This makes life seem magical, fun, and full of moments of enlightenment, illumination, and spiritual direction. For example, this morning my daily reflection from the *Science of Mind* magazine's Daily Guides was on Gratitude. As I was reading through it I suddenly recalled that I had woken up from sleep last night rather abruptly, and I was saying loudly, "THANK you, Lord, THANK you . . . I AM SO GRATEFUL." This gratitude feeling just bubbled out in sleep and washed over me. I have much to ponder on this incident, a message delivered, one not to be ignored . . . my knowing that there are no random happenings, no coincidences, only events pregnant with hidden meaning.

Having some vague notion of wanting something in the future that will bring us happiness is like eating a whole meal of cotton candy and waiting to feel satisfied and filled up. It'll never happen. You'll be sick before you are full. To feel purposeful, intentional, powerful with a definite knowing and surety that what you wish for is already on its way to fulfillment, you must name it, claim it, and believe it.

What gets in the way of this powerfully positive divine process is the notion, perhaps buried deep down inside us ready to sabotage our dreams, that we really are not worthy of the happiness we seek. Or that we put such restrictions and detailed parameters around the wish or desire that we don't recognize it when its right in front of us . . . hidden in plain sight. Naming, claiming, asserting, affirming, believing, receiving, enjoying, creating, changing, ascending, expanding, loving, growing, experiencing . . . all these are yours when you know you are a spiritual being having a human experience.

WHEN I WAS YOUNGER, in my late teens and early twenties, if someone would have asked me what was my fondest wish for myself, my ultimate, best life that I would want to be leading, the happiest and most satisfying place within myself . . . I would not have been able to articulate any kind of an answer because, as I see it now, those questions were not even available to me to ask myself. I was just too practical in my thinking . . . if it's not doable, or seems not possible or achievable, has no well-laid out plan or path to succeeding, then I would discount or dismiss it from my mind and get back to work on what was in front of me.

If something was hidden in plain sight I had a tendency to overlook it, and its value to me in the moment would then be lost. I had a good life in my earlier years . . . they were just constructed of practical problems and meeting them with practical solutions, squeezing some of the fun out of my life then lived, replacing it with seriousness and responsibility and, in a way, survival. More joyful living was to show up later in my life, as I met fellow travelers.

It seems that most times the brilliance of our own ideas, our creativity, the moments of our personal inspiration and enlightenment, go unacknowledged and uncelebrated, not by others but by ourselves. We may not see in ourselves our latent gifts and abilities, our talents just beneath the surface of our consciousness, hovering about among our hopes and dreams, our aspirations, and our heartfelt wishes. These do not have to be Fourth of July-style "Aha" moments, but may be quiet contemplations, a recapitulation of the day's events, the interactions, the problem-solving, the celebration of life in small moments one on one with someone. It does require us to acknowledge our worthwhileness, to name it so it can live and breathe and become a part of who we are, a confidence in one's own ability to affect other people in a positive and life-giving way. It is in moments of reflection and self-celebration that we begin to see our emerging gifts, our latent talents, our burning desires for building a world that works for all of us.

A powerful but elusive practice is to allow thoughts to enter into one's mind and then be released without judgment, a kind of thought awareness, a momentary recognition, a turning over in one's mind . . . an examination and then a letting go. This is all done inside the process called "meditation" . . . within a suitable setting where introspection and reflection can occur.

Instead of having a set place and a set time, I like to open myself to the possibility that epiphany moments and enlightenment, creative ideas, illuminating insights, energy infusions ahead of some radical right action, are the payoffs of meditation, and these pearls of potentiality can occur at any time of the day or night, in any situation or circumstance, under any conditions . . . then powerfully fueled with wakefulness and awareness, in every moment, your life can expand beyond your fondest dreams; vistas of high possibility open before you; you begin to see things differently and to view yourself in a new light as well, becoming a powerful change-agent in the world.

OUTSIDE OURSELVES, cycles of life in nature are occurring all around us, some more noticeable and dramatic to us: sunrises, sunsets, the first blooms of spring, that first snow of winter, the last sigh of summer as leaves change color and trees give up their foliage . . . each of us in our knowing and our experience see and feel these cycles of life in our own way. But what of our inner person, our soul-self? Are we not also cycling and moving through life . . . between contraction and expansion, from embracing to letting go, from finding to losing, from lucidity to confusion, from fear to freedom . . . coming to completions and crossing new thresholds, doors opening, doors closing, life birthing, life ending?

We can choose to be awake and aware to all of it in each present moment, for it brings signs and signals, guideposts and stop signs, forks in the road . . . to help us go deeper into our discernment, to ponder meaning amidst paradoxes and uncertainties, to learn to love the notion that change is inevitable and answers are found by going to the Divine Within Us, to the God which changes not.

Oh, to be congruent, consistent, honest, to have integrity in all one's dealings is to be at peace, to experience deep, abiding tranquility . . . modeling and nurturing the divine qualities that we were made from. If we say one thing and do another, have hidden agendas, deceive by our actions, openly or hidden away as fear, anger or judgment, defying the congruity of our true nature, we are out of integrity and our self-esteem begins to waiver. We are out of balance, out of round.

We must be willing to honestly look at ourselves, to hang with people who are modeling God's best and brightest hopes for us. By fostering an inner environment of self-love, we find equanimity, a greater acceptance. Then, in the midst of chaos and incongruity, compassion and forgiveness reign supreme as our natural responses. Love the world even as external situations shift and change. Whatever happens, we now have a new relationship with it; we embrace it. We are okay with it. We have accommodated it and adapted it to our own inner spiritual style.

If we could only remind ourselves once in awhile that life is a process, a series of moments to be enjoyed, celebrated, learned from. The pearls of insight, enlightenment, illumination, and divine guidance can enter into our conscious thinking if we just focus on being present to what is in front of us. Our lists, schedules, and calendars are fine for planning purposes, but being lost in the moment, not aware of the passage of time, pleasurably wrapped up and lost in who we are at that moment has to be the best use of our time allowed to us on Earth. Yesterday, I spent four hours at a preschool, one on one and in small groups, creating artifacts and drawing pictures, reading stories, working puzzles, connecting with individual students in ways I had not experienced previously . . . marvelous discoveries of "big souls with short legs," their individual personalities, backgrounds, ethnicities, all of us bonding and blending in a beautiful dance of life . . . time passed quickly and I only glanced at my watch once in the four hours.

There is in each of us the still, small voice quietly urging us to follow our bliss, to be in the world, gifting the world with our authentic self. From Rumi, a Persian Sufi mystic and poet: "Let yourself be silently drawn by the strange pull of what you really love. It will not lead you astray." For me, I need only look back along the path of my life's journey to come to the conclusion that I have been, at each step of the way, following my bliss, instinctually and intuitively moving through life, sometimes in survival mode, other times in the flow of life, celebrating and enjoying what was in front of me. It continues to be a magical and miracle-filled process for me: persons arriving, persons leaving, events unfolding, circumstances creating, synchronicities revealing, coincidences occurring, enlightenments illuminating, teachers inspiring, children striving, way-showers leading, I myself listening, learning, discerning, believing, receiving, affirming, expanding, growing, feeling, doing, being all that I can be . . . all this I can see clearly now, and I am blessed.

CHOICES HAVE A WAY OF creating our experiences, and the accumulation of our choices through life becomes our story. Looking back on our choices may give us a powerful tool to see more clearly the road we have taken to get where we are, and to illuminate that authentic being within, which we then can embrace and appreciate as having been with us, guiding and guarding us, giving us directions where and how to go or not to go, every step of our going.

For my own part, I can see clearly that my studying for the priesthood and then abandoning it as a calling established in me the desire to be useful to people, to be of sacred service, to be in the presence of children . . . which surfaced later in my life as a calling to be a volunteer in elementary and middle schools . . . to participate in life through serving the needs of children . . . so the feeling of failure that was deep in me at the time I returned to the secular world remained as a candle of consciousness waiting to be relit and redirected into useful and sacred service in a way I could never have imagined would be played out in my later life.

I can see clearly now that making the decision to volunteer after high school graduation for three years of service in the U.S. Army gave me the incentive to not waste any more time after being discharged, but to immediately enroll in college, get my education, get on with my life, after it had been on hold for three years, and to take my place as a productive member of society . . . to powerfully move on.

Today I am grateful for just being alive, able to take nourishment, breathe the fresh, invigorating air of freedom, and be of useful service. Having just had my annual physical, I know that all my pieces and parts are good to go for another year. I used this checkpoint of my health and general condition of my well-being as a sign or signal as to how I should proceed into the next phase; a general slowing down, or revving up, or just maintaining status quo, steady as I go. I am so grateful to feel that I am given the green light to follow my bliss much as before but to tweak it and alter it so as to keep life interesting, responsive to new challenges and opportunities to serve, to be useful, and to make a difference in the lives of the most needy and vulnerable among us. I need not look to the past for the best of times nor to the future hoping to achieve some distant elusive goal, but to the present moment pregnant with high potential and unlimited possibilities to serve the greater good, influence the course of some young person's life to their betterment . . . making this a better world for all.

I have been most fortunate that through the years, when crisis or calamity has entered my life to threaten my stability, my security, or try to take away my most precious values of family, my self-worth, my usefulness, I seem to cope and continue to strive forward by calling on my inner reserve of resolve and the fortitude to carry on, to rise above, to shake off the shackles of discontent, foreboding, or any feeling of permanent loss, enough so that I see myself recovering, returning to being that whole person again.

I have always been able to land on my feet, able to look forward rather than backward, look around me and see everything and everyone that is propping me up, raising me out of the malaise of my discontent, and I recall and remember all those upon whose shoulders I stood as I wavered and waffled at the crossroads of crisis in my life. I am grateful in my remembering their strength and their gifts of compassionate understanding. Armed with renewed strength and vigor, enthusiastic for the living out of my own life in loving-kindness and compassionate service to others, I push on, and I run life's race with confidence.

Watching movies with superheroes like Superman and Batman battling crime, saving ordinary people, getting in and out of tough situations but always "saving the day," looked to me like extremely exhausting and sometimes thankless work just trying to be all things to all people. When did they ever have time for themselves, I wondered. Perhaps in our own lifetimes, we have jumped into other people's personal circumstances fully intending to be that element that picks the person up and carries them off to safety, and perhaps we have to do this again and again . . . this other person getting a free ride but never experiencing that teaching moment where they stand on their own two feet, emotionally and a little tougher mentally.

IN MY LIFE, I HAVE SEEN myself as protector, provider, capable, congruent, consistent, authentic, law-abiding, role model to hundreds of someone else's children. I have burdened myself with unneeded concern and worry in having the responsibility for others when it was time for them to jump off the cliff and grow their own wings. I am a work-in-progress, to let go and let God in these areas.

Yogi Berra, the much-beloved baseball icon who was a catcher for the New York Yankees, had an expression that sounded definitive and certain in providing sage advice, but in the end left you hanging, unresolved and still looking for answers. It goes like this: "When you come to a fork in the road, take it." Doesn't it leave you just where you started, if you're looking for Divine Guidance? It all comes back to you, your intuitive nature, your experiences, how you see yourself interacting with the Divine Intelligence always standing ready to guide and to guard us through any situation when we come to a fork in the road. Making choices does not always require us to be spontaneous, looking in control, reactive nor immediate in our response when finding a fork in the road. It can be a good thing, a time to pause, take stock and take inventory of one's life, take time out to assess and go within . . . the universe has your next step waiting for you . . . to be revealed in due course . . . in its own good time.

I know that miracles are happening all around me on a regular basis, within my understanding, or clouded and opaque, outside my ability to comprehend. The degree to which I can look for clarity from within, trusting my intuitive soul-self for guidance, I can navigate the slippery slopes and turbulent, tossing seas of day-to-day challenges and infinite possibilities, to come finally at rest to see more clearly that which has gone before me in life, that which is happening now, and that which will forever be my future path and direction, itself operating from a place that has never experienced loss, limitation, lack, or fear . . . a realm of abundance, light and the infinite possibility and unlimited potentiality of miracles occurring on a regular basis, within and around me and I can use their power and energy to turn my world around . . . miraculously and magnificently for myself and everyone else. Should I only believe, then I will see such miracles operating in my life, bringing me my greatest good.

What were the times when you confronted the pitfalls and road blocks of complacency and careless living to experience a breakthrough into the higher realm of your greatest good? Mac Davis in these song lyrics certainly personified and captured the attitude of someone not quite ready to have that epiphany moment of self-realization that there's got to be something better out there for me and it's up to me to grasp it and be it:

> "Oh Lord it's hard to be humble
> When you're perfect in every way
> I can't wait to look in the mirror
> Cause I get better looking each day..."

My moments of illumination and enlightenment, my epiphany moments when I said "no more," came slowly and painfully as I continually refused to face the reality that I was slowly self-destructing and distancing myself from any meaningful relationship with all that I held dear in my life. When I walked away from the need for alcohol to prop me up and give me courage, however false and fleeting, I got my life back,

I looked at those around me with fresh eyes and deeper love. I got my life back and along with it, my self-respect.

When I made the decision to give up drinking alcohol, I did not have to delve into the whys and the wherefores of how I had gotten to this point of departure or what was wrong in my life that showed up as a dependency and a necessity to becoming my drink of choice, each and every time. All I knew was that it had me and that I had lost my freedom of choice, and this I did not like. It was perfectly proper in the context of my social and business life to "hoist a few" with friends or business associates, but when it became the "go-to" beverage when I was by myself, then I began to see how it was setting me apart and isolating me from those I loved the most, my family. At first, being on the road with business associates or in family gatherings, each where alcohol was a staple, set me apart and was somewhat awkward in my first instances of refusing to drink, but after a while people accepted my action as "that's just Roger," and I slipped into obscurity without feeling I had lost something irretrievably valuable, that I never really missed it. I took one for the team.

DID YOU EVER FEEL truly worthy of rest and relaxation, not because you earned it but because you were honoring the signs and signals that your body just wished to slow down and be restful for awhile? Guilt for being motionless and still can be a hard feeling to overcome in our go-go culture, which prizes activity and getting things done. The dark side of this constant need to be doing is the heavy responsibility we start to associate with our productivity, our value to others, our usefulness . . . fueled by the feeling that we are never quite enough.

The worst manifestation of this "busyness" spiraling syndrome of activity is feeling that one can never be sick or not at one's very best at all times, a natural outcome when feeling the heavy weight of personal, professional, and family responsibility. There were times in my life when I felt uncovered, exposed to outside circumstances, overwhelmed, inadequate to step up to fill some greater need . . . when someone significant in my life passed away . . . and again at work when someone above me left the company, and I was left to fill the gap that had been created.

Have we ever dragged ourselves through a difficult, unpleasant experience only to find in the end that the situation became a powerful teaching moment or redirected us on a path more suitable for who we are and what we were to become in the world? Perhaps these realizations have come as epiphany moments, or quantum leaps of illumination, or in baby steps of hesitancy and uncertainty, only gaining confidence and courage little by little as we observe, take in, and respond to the passing scene before us.

AS AN EIGHTH GRADER in a Catholic school, an altar boy, and one securely ensconced and immersed in the teachings of the church, I answered the call to become a priest. For three years on into high school, I studied and worked as a seminarian on the road to the priesthood. I admired and wished for the bonding and connection I had seen between our parish priest and the children of our school. I left the seminary after only a few years of study, returned to the secular world, but am now fulfilling that deep desire of connection with children, those who are the neediest and most vulnerable among us, as a school volunteer.

I have never had too much trouble staying positive even in the worst of situations or the most dire of times in my life. I have never had a hopeless feeling of "no way out;" somehow the wheels kept churning even when solutions did not clearly present themselves. Epiphany moments of being illuminated with wisdom and correct ways of going never was how I moved out of tough situations, into safe harbors, and then to solution and resolution. It was more a partnering with my soul-self, an underlying confidence not always realizing its powerful presence, pushing forward, armed with such intuitive powers and survival instincts as to weather every storm and come out the other side, having grown in character, resolve, path illuminated, eager and enthusiastic to get on with my life. I can recall and recount the dark moments, the dark nights of my soul in my life, but I don't wish to do that. I am too full of worthwhile endeavors populating my horizon, projects and plans that make me feel useful and purposeful, people to meet, child-whispering to do, my life to be lived fully, abundantly, magnificently well.

Panic, fear, and high anxiety have visited very few times in my life, and for this I am grateful. One recurring sense of panic and foreboding happened in my early elementary school years when the group was reading in class and I just did not want to be called on to read in front of the class. I envision now that I tried then to hide behind the person in front of me and not be noticed. I suspect that kind of feeling carried over into my corporate career when I always over-prepared and re-rehearsed my presentations to management. I always knew my stuff, but looking back it seemed like a high price to pay to try to be perfect in my business performances.

Today as a school volunteer, I teach classes of elementary students the Junior Great Books curriculum. I read chapter books to whole classrooms of students during their snack break; many of my teacher-directed assignments are handed to me without any prior preparation or warning, and I just go with the flow, and it all works out well. When you are following your bliss, loving what you do, feeling useful and impactful, you are living your best life.

MORE THAN TEN YEARS AGO, I was stepping through the door of metaphysics and radical techniques of self-improvement and enlightened thinking. I was greeted by the philosophy and writings of Caroline Myss, which resonated so strongly with me that it made me look at things differently and put me on a never-to-turn-back path of self-discovery, showing me outlets and fostering deeper dreams for my gifts and resources to be useful and life-changing to others. The thread of experiences throughout my life was culminating in the radical belief that I had been put on this Earth to be a servant of sacred service to those most needy and most vulnerable among us, and I was led to wish to spend the rest of my days "in the presence of children." This was the phrase that kept coming back to me, naming my destiny, and framing the specific direction I was to take in my life . . . and from that time on after saying "yes" to it, situations and circumstances, people and events, spontaneous occurrences, magical moments, serendipitous happenings, personal awakenings all illumined my path, infused me, and enthused me with courage and energy to follow my bliss.

Looking back on my early childhood years, I had a sense that there was a certain dysfunctional aspect occurring around me that I did not feel safe in or want to be a part of. So in the environment of mixed signals of love and aberrant behavior patterns, I went about my life constructing walls of solitary behavior, not sharing with others the interest I had in my school work, in my athletic accomplishments, or in my hopes and dreams. There was safety inside this carefully constructed and well-managed daily existence, but the give-up was that there was no room for spontaneity, freedom to be the me inside of me, more guarded and introspective than a child growing up should be.

My main driving incentive of the heart was: I did not want to fall short in the eyes of my loved ones; I wanted above all, to be liked, to please, and not to be judged as falling short; to be shunned or ignored by others was a continuing shadow over me that drove me to seek approval through being useful and successful in my later life. I have come out of these dark moments, still carrying some of their burden but lighter and a better person for it.

During the times in my life when I have been ill or recovering from surgery or just forced to go offline from my daily activities, two strong and persistent feelings have dominated my recovery periods. First, I felt I was letting my teachers at the school down by not being there to follow through on my volunteer obligations. The specter of always wanting to please, always the strong one, never disappointing, pulling my weight, not needing to depend on others . . . loomed yet again in my life. And second, I missed doing my work, that which made me feel useful, productive, worthy and that which I loved to do, was being withheld from me during my recovery periods. Sometimes you discover what is most important to you when it is taken away, even if for only a little while.

It is a good thing to be blessed with being able to do something that is useful to others and that you love to do, and maybe it even reaches the level of your calling, your destiny. I am so grateful for being able to walk around in that blissful feeling of knowing and using my gifts to help the most needy and the most vulnerable in our midst, the children.

CAN YOU BRING YOURSELVES TO BELIEVE that the peace and happiness you are seeking is also seeking you; that the universe is conspiring to give you what you wish for and in doing so, it is important to focus on the positive things we want and not on the things we wish to avoid? As we believe what we perceive, so shall that be what we receive. So simple, yet it takes practice . . . being almost serendipitous, serene, smiling, sure that life is sending your way all that your hopes and dreams have been wanting to tell you. You are what you believe you are.

I never knew that I could transform myself from a corporate cash-manager, office-dweller type to a radical believer that I had the gifts, enthusiasm, and the power to be a child-whisperer, to engage the youngest among us at their level of being, connecting intuitively at their place of need, not only for learning lessons in school, but filling a place in their hearts that speaks to them of my caring deeply for their personhood, their deepest core selves, and just dwelling in the delight of exploring their joyous and carefree selves, their sometimes reckless abandon.

I am at my happiest first thing in the morning, savoring the gifts of quietude and noiseless, non-demands on my time . . . I open my daily inspirational guides, pen in hand, and I begin to scribe the words and thoughts of that day's way-shower and spiritual teacher. Words penned on paper open me up to receive inspiration, guidance, and ways of looking at things differently. Scribing is not original, but I long ago dismissed that negative thought from my mind. With books at my side, I seek out and bring in to this divine communication, quotes, sayings, sage advice of other way-showers and thought leaders. Together it all weaves a mosaic of magical moments completely original in its construction and extremely instructive and forward-impelling for my day.

After years of this sacred process unfolding, scribing, assimilating, creating from the works of others, I have opened myself to accompany this work with my own self-made composition of random but inspired self-dialogue, wisdom pieces from the depth of my soul-self.

It is difficult to continue to feel you are responsible for every action, every ramification, every choice, every situation that confronts those who are in our circle of loving and caring . . . and also take care of ourselves, always projecting to the outside world a mask of competence, wisdom, and ability to weather any storms on our life's path. That is a heavy load of responsibility to carry. The extreme of this misplaced assignment, self-inflicted, to be all things to all people, comes through when someone else suffers a tragedy, and you wish it were you rather than them; or, worse yet, when someone dies, and you feel guilty that you survived. If this deceased person was part of your inner circle of love and their transition was a heavy blow to others in your group, your first reaction might be thoughts like, "I can't get sick now . . . if something happens to me, I couldn't bear that my loved ones should suffer another loss." Misguided as that is, we must know that we are all guided and guarded by Divine Intelligence and that we must press on knowing we have work to do and miles to go.

When I was first "washed up on the shore" of Mile Hi Church one Sunday morning, I did not realize then as I do now that I was in for a life-changing, soul-rendering, mind-boggling experience. I don't know if my eyes were wide open in amazed disbelief, but I did know that my heart and mind were joined in wonderment at what was happening in that church. I was engulfed in music and words and with people all around me, all of which resounded in my ears and in my heart . . . I knew I had finally come home. It was a feeling that came as close to being the biblical prodigal son as I could get. That day I was embraced by a transformational experience that was so intense that it has taken all of these eight years since to absorb and to respond to its promptings by saying, "What do I do with this now?" I have now surrounded myself with the most positive, spirit-led, inner-directed, good-hearted, open-armed beings I could have never imagined existed before my day of epiphany and illumination. I am so blessed. I just want to give back all that I can, and to go on giving.

IT USED TO BE IMPORTANT to me to have my day planned out . . . efficient, calculated, no surprises. Even my leisure activities, like golf . . . it was always "practice with a purpose." It felt good to have structure, no wasted action, attached firmly to the outcome, and everything in between was necessary to get to some finish line. I was secure and safe in this self-made predictable process, and it held me in good stead, keeping the lows from getting too low but also muting and modifying the high points, squeezing out the exhilaration and joy of the moment. Things, they are a'changing . . . people and circumstances have shown up that have lightened me up, loosened me up, not so much moving into more fun and frivolity . . . but opening me up to allow space for the unexpected, the unusual, the unanticipated, the mystery and magic to surprise and delight me, to challenge me, to stretch me, and to hone my skills and gifts to take me down the yellow brick road of self-discovery, expansion, new vistas, to greater glory.

In my journey from corporate manager to school volunteer and with stops in between to pause, stumble, fall, and pick myself up, each time a different, enlightened, and emergent self, I have discovered I am now living the life I was made for, expressly capable of and gifted with magical powers and the imagination to stimulate and motivate, to energize, and to awaken that self-same response from the children I serve in sacred service. I have gone from a childhood desire to not be a burden to my struggling family, to being useful as a young contributing adolescent, and then as a young man independent and free to move about in the wider world, to survive and to thrive in my own way . . . to then move into the world of servant leadership, volunteerism, larger usefulness (reviving my childhood desire), now ascending into realms of being impactful in the lives of children, taking personal risks to expose my skills in classrooms, working with the competency of teachers far better educated to teach than me, realizing I can do this . . . the "this" being a discovery of my gifts and leveraging my abilities to make a difference in the lives of the most needy and vulnerable among us, the children.

It is obvious that as we look around our homes, we have given in, time and time again, to the urge to hoard in the hidden recesses, closets, and basements an accumulation of what at one time seemed precious and special to us, but that now lies silent and sullen, stuffed away, tarnished and tawdry, ignored and inefficient for our current cravings and

purposes. Running in parallel is our marvelously constructed consciousness and mindset, processing, storing, sorting, keeping, and accumulat-
ing clutters of thoughts, feelings, beliefs, and plans . . . plans for fixing
that which appears to be broken or not working, plans to start on some
new pathways of purposeful pursuits, some concrete and definite, some
whimsical and fancifully abiding in the fairy-tale castle of our brain, to
be taken out occasionally, enjoyed, and put back, not to be acted on . . .
how to sort it all out, to make sense of it, to find purpose and meaning
for our desires, our longings, those impulsive intrusions into our mind .
. . the Creative Divine Intelligence of the universe stands ready to provide clarity and direction, should we just turn to It for help.

TODAY WORDS AND PHRASES are coming at me seemingly from all
directions, at first glance unrelated to each other, but opening my mind's
eye and putting me in a posture to receive without immediately understanding their connection. They begin to coalesce and conjoin into
more meaningful messages of magnificent potentiality for my life, and
I am eager to use it all. The first to appear to me is: "There is guidance
for each of us, and by lowly listening, we shall hear the right word"
(Ralph Waldo Emerson). "When the student is ready, the teacher will
appear" (Buddha). And perhaps the most obscure, but I'm sure with
some powerful message for me: "Sell your cleverness, and buy bewil-
derment" (Rumi).

Within myself I carry the seeds of discernment to clarify and
discover all that is being said to me through the voices of others, my
own processing and thinking self, assimilating, organizing, codifying,

illuminating, visioning, enlightening my soul-self to look backwards and see clearly now how people and events have conspired to create the story of my life and how this is all going to be used and useful to create, ongoing, a better world and me in the middle of it all, playing a significant part.

Decluttering techniques have become all the rage to rid ourselves of once wanted but now burdensome stacks of this and racks of that, weighing us down as we move from one phase of life into another, unable to get sufficient traction both mentally and physically to push ahead into our greater yet to be. And heaven forbid we let any friends down into our basement for any reason whatsoever! A family member sends this decluttering technique from the sacred Buddhist tradition to assist us: "Just go around your house and hold the things you have accumulated for just a moment; if you do not feel a spark of joy as you hold them, throw them away." He tried it and so far he has only thrown away the vegetables in his refrigerator and his electric bill.

Decluttering has its practical benefits of passing on to those most needy that which we use no more. The bigger payoff is creating an invitation for the universe to fill our empty mind spaces with enlightened new direction, renewed vigor and energy, insights for new beginnings, discovering opportunities for service and usefulness all in plain sight, awaiting our recognition.

MANY OF US WERE BROUGHT UP TO BELIEVE that the pie was only so big and you had to work hard to get your share of limited opportunities. This feeling of lack and limitation was confirmed on a daily basis by external economic news and negative world events impinging on our personal world. Health issues, relationship challenges, marital break-ups, uncertainties, and unstable conditions on the work front led to worries of job security and continued employment. This all certainly held in check any reaching out and desiring greater experiences and the finer things of life.

Now comes New Thought teachings in the midst of all this discontent and stubborn have-not-ism. Now come spiritual leaders and way-showers creating the framework and the groundwork for believing, then receiving the message of positivity—that unlimited possibilities and infinite opportunities lay not before us but within us, only to be activated as we conceive and believe that if we are doing our right work, following our brightest stars, we surely will be living our best lives.

I never really liked dwelling on the past. Regrets for not having done something, or having done something that now cannot be undone, can be painful and pointless, and a heavy load to carry around into the chores and challenges of the present day. I gain positive momentum and enthusiasm for the prospects that lay before me by simply jotting down a brief outlined schedule of events and happenings, which generally doesn't get altered through the course of my day's school volunteer activities. The possibility of risk and unknowns coming into my work is taken away by my having a good, sturdy, structured schedule.

In my later years I have realized that rigidity and preparedness push away surprises, serendipitous moments, spontaneity, and just plain pleasure of thinking on one's feet when confronted by surprises, and kids in school are full of ways to knock your thinking off balance. So in my planning calendar, I have learned to leave mind-space for the unpredicted, the unforeseen, the unexpected and then go with the flow and enjoy the moment.

There is a term in fishing parlance called "catch and release." For the pure joy of fishing, one catches a fish not to eat it, but to enjoy the process, the competition, the interplay between man and nature in its own element, and then returns the fish to its natural habitat, unharmed, and, if it can be, happy and grateful to be released. Suppose we think of the fish as dark thoughts swimming about in the deeper waters of our minds, ever lurking, ever ready to suffocate and sabotage our hopes, our dreams . . . even our daily plans and activities. And suppose we need help from the outside—affirmative prayer, practitioner experience, spiritual mind treatment—to lift us from the dark night of the soul, from being caught in a spiral of angst and anxiety.

But then with what can only be called support from a benign and compassionate universe, we have an epiphany moment, an enlightenment, an illumination, a divine revelation, a way out of the morass, and behold, at one time we were caught, and now we are released to move on into our greatest-yet-to-become.

An embarrassing, red-in-the-face, "oh no" kind of thought occasionally comes to me as I step over, step around, step through the clutter in my closet, to reach deep into the desultorily cast discards of yesteryear . . . to reach for that one, old, dear, familiar piece of clothing that is first choice to me, day in and day out. What am I doing, holding onto who knows what for whatever reason, long gone as having any meaning or purpose whatsoever. And should I transition suddenly, is it my parting shot to suffer others, who were just unlucky enough to be around at my passing, to have to deal with all my stuff whose glory days have gone, or never were, decipher, sift through, ponder over, carry out, discard, or devise various ways to pound usefulness back into that which hangs on hangers, is stashed in boxes, hidden in dark places, some gems among the junk, some items to be kept, wept over, memories kept with meaning for the keeper. It is all a hodgepodge of opportunity . . . but why not do it now, lay it on the one who made the clutter, find the gems in it all, and then move on.

If one's head be filled with the stuff of dreams and schemes and faraway images of the brightest and most wonderful things, is there a chance, perchance, that one could overshoot the mark and fall far beyond the land of opportunity, the place that needs your spark? And if we be like the Walrus and the Carpenter walking across the land thinking "the beach was wide from side to side, but much too full of sand," talking on and on of "cabbage and kings, and while the sea is hot, whether pigs have wings." By shooting too far beyond what stands in need in front of us to be addressed, are we missing the chance to use our gifts and show our very best?

AS A YOUNG MAN barely out of my teens, I had seen much of what was the best and worst in the world of human behavior, and it occurred on some pretty wide stages like many parts of the United States and even in some European countries. I had it in my mind that with all this rich travel experience I could somehow see myself on the international scene, perhaps in the U.S. Diplomatic Corps, working in a foreign embassy. After taking a few foreign language courses in college, this unlikeliest of dreams vanished amidst the need to find real employment after graduation.

I can see clearly now that there has been a chain of circumstances, situations, people coming and going in my life, influencing me both positively and not so positively, creating the mosaic of my moments pieced together into the story of my life. Superimposed upon these externals has been my own personality, my own inclinations, my own intuitive disposition to view the world in a certain way and to go in the direction that suited me the best. Although I was not stubborn in demeanor as a kid, nor a problem child in almost all respects, when push came to shove I knew which way I needed/wanted to go, and I moved swiftly and decisively. I was blessed with parents who, even though most times could not figure out how or why I thought the way I did, stood by, shrugging shoulders in resignation, and allowing me to evolve into my own person.

So the challenges I brought to my parents were the results of the independent action and decisions I made: to study for the priesthood, go to St. Gregory High School, join the Army, go to Michigan State University—all on my own volition without parental input, but always with what I felt were their silent if bewildered blessings.

Looking back on my upbringing, living in a city of more than four million people of every color, creed, religious persuasion, coming from every walk in life imaginable, I moved about the city of Chicago amongst them all, yes, knowing there were differences between and among all those I met or passed by in my daily living. I took public transportation (bus, elevated train, subway) to go to high school and to visit my friends who did not live in my neighborhood. We were a far flung band of loyal young renegades, willing to make that extra effort to hang together. Joining the Army I was further flung into the midst of every sort of humanity as men from everywhere were trained into a cohesive military unit. And Michigan State University kept exposing me to a greater diversity of people, thoughts, and lifestyles.

It all taught me to appreciate and respect the differences in people, and now since I have been "washed up on shore" of Mile Hi Church, I am able to find a way to celebrate and acknowledge joyfully the oneness and wholeness of all peoples, to genuinely love our uniqueness and what makes us individuals. And I can see clearly now that my past life prepared me powerfully and well to embrace the wider world.

SOMEWHERE ALONG OUR PATH in life, our human condition will be confronted with seemingly insurmountable circumstances, challenges to our beliefs, doubts as to our ability to overcome that which has entered our lives and disrupted our state of blissful happiness. As Dorothy said, "Toto, we aren't in Kansas anymore." At some point serendipity is overtaken by reality, and we are shaken from our lethargy into our battle stations, knowing our very essence is being threatened. However described or felt, we have all been there or else we are living in a dream world of our own making.

Starting with the steadfast belief that in everything we have a choice, we are armed with a faith that we can always look at circumstances in our life from a different point of view. Gathering additional powerful thoughts, we remind ourselves that we are not alone but that an omnipresent, attentive, all-powerful universe stands ready to act on the wishes and desires our thoughts have invoked. We have a choice to be courageous and lead ourselves out of the labyrinth and entanglement of dead-end thinking into the light and illumination of divine intervention for our greater good.

Being attached to outcomes of how we think our lives should be going can bring frustration, impatience, and an intolerant attitude of non-acceptance for what is confronting us and blocking our feelings of well-being. Six years ago the "Just For Girls" program at the local recreation center was a nonstarter. I knew the idea of it: to bring resources and programs to young girls, empowering them to make better lifestyle and healthier choices, was a good one.... Now it is a thriving, flourishing, ongoing activity reaching many of our young women. It is now a "living idea" that took time to take root and grow.

Similar in personal impact, I have submitted an application to volunteer at the Children's Cancer Hospital . . . talking to the coordinator, I was told it might take months to process and act on my application. How could I miss being considered with 800 hours a year of volunteer service at a local K-8 school to beef up my resume? I am entangled in my own high estimation of my volunteer value, seeing myself as indispensable, and wondering why others can't see me that way immediately. It is now time for me to put all in the hands of Divine Intelligence and wait for further instructions.

At the age of fourteen, I already knew what I wanted in life, and that was to be a priest of God. I had been an altar boy for four years prior and felt this was my calling. It felt good to be so certain, so right about something . . . to have my path laid out, to be a person in such a prestigious and useful profession . . . a way of helping others, and at the same time saving my soul with my ticket punched for Heaven . . . and, of course, my parents were proud of me for my decision. I was thrown together with a sea of 1,300 seminarians to swim for our lives upstream through the curriculum of Greek, Latin, math, science, and religion for eleven years, and then to deposit us, ordained as priests, on the shores of some unsuspecting but welcoming parish, which looked upon we novices as the final word in dogma and scripture espoused by the Catholic Church. Did I mention that out of the 1,300 eager seminarians who start this process, eleven years later, about twenty-five are ordained as priests? . . . But we were undaunted, we band of Carpe Diem hopefuls; but alas, I was a casualty after two-and-a-half years of seminary life and assimilated myself back into secular society to carry my hopes and desires out into the wider world of human endeavor.

A popular practice among highly introspective and reflective people is to recapitulate in mind before going to bed the events of the day and weigh how circumstances and situations were handled, what went well or less well, and generally end up with a feeling that, on balance, lessons were learned and the day was positively lived and contributions made. Beyond this overview of the day's activities, there is a way of thinking at the point of action or reaction in a particular situation that allows us an element of control and an opportunity to make the best decisions for ourselves and others in the moment.

It is the presence of a witness within ourselves that, when used at the pause-point between a stimulating event and our response to it, we can perceive without reacting, weigh and evaluate alternatives, conceive a plan of right action that creates the greatest good for ourselves and factors in how our actions will bring the highest and best for others. This powerful witnessing concept, brought to us in the teachings of Deepak Chopra, is just another way to see life, circumstances, and the world around us differently for the common good.

In our secular society, we have come to measure our worth and esteem by how successfully we navigate the often uncertain and daunting hurdles and pitfalls life deals out to us. We are happy or sad depending on our level of security and safety in what often appears as an unfriendly and unforgiving world. Our striving many times does not lead us to outcomes that satisfy our needs, and so we remain restless and unfulfilled, falling short, never being quite enough to satisfy ourselves or those whose opinions count most to us. There is a greater life principle gaining support among New Age way-showers and thought leaders that all we should need or want is already inside ourselves . . . that our attachment to outcomes, how it all will look in the end, fixates and limits the greater potential and possibilities waiting to be birthed and manifested for our greater good. To quote Ernest Holmes, "There are hidden powers, undeveloped resources, unimaginable depths of our being that we can penetrate and bring to the surface and make our personality anything we wish it to be."

I ALWAYS APPROACHED LIFE situations and changing conditions with the idea that if I made a plan or injected some degree of certainty into the outcome, all things would fall into place, and I would be all right in the end. Life-altering decisions—like becoming a priest, going into the Army, selecting a college, choosing a livelihood, being married, building a family, changing jobs, buying homes, choosing to retire, taking up volunteering at schools as a life choice, moving from one state to another and another and another—in all of this, deep down I had a courageous heart telling me it was OK, even though on the surface I may have been full of misgivings and trepidation, particularly when things got rolling and the actual facts of the situation began to reveal themselves. Misgivings, yes, but no regrets or "shouldas, wouldas, couldas." Once I stepped over the line of commitment I was all in. I think that helped the people in my life affected by my decisions and inclinations to stay the course with me. I have been blessed with all things necessary to move through tough times and changes.

If the stock market, specifically the Dow Jones Industrial Average, were to drop 600+ points in one day, and at the same time, your beloved Chicago Cubs just finished a four-game losing streak, after having forty wins and only twenty losses in the first two months of the baseball season . . . would your entire belief system of thinking you were safe and secure, untouchable by any imaginable situation or chain of events be shaken to the core and conjure up in your mind doom and gloom, more badness yet to come, pull up the stakes, batten down the hatches, or as Bette Davis said in the movie *All About Eve*, "Fasten your seatbelts; it's going to be a bumpy night"? From time to time our beliefs are challenged, their validity questioned, thoughts of abandoning or replacing them conjured up in our minds, but usually such storms are weathered, the sun comes out again, the inner voice advising you to throw in the towel is not listened to . . . and we come out the other side intact, better for the experience, more staunch and stalwart, trusting and tougher in our belief that we can prevail, carry on, and do good work for those whom we meet on our path.

Looking back in time and having 20/20 hindsight I can see clearly how people and events have shaped, directed, influenced, and modeled for me how I should act, react, respond to, deal with, and triumph over all situations and circumstances I have confronted on my path. I like the idea that there is a universe out there, omnipresent and divinely intelligent, which assists and responds to our ideas, hopes, wants, and dreams as we direct it to do so . . . a powerful co-creating companion in the construction of the stories of our lives. All the experiences created from our choices are imbedded firmly in our subconscious minds as what we believe to be our world of reality. From our belief system comes our way of relating and being. As Mahatma Gandhi said, "Your beliefs become your thoughts, your thoughts become your words, your words become your actions, your actions become your habits, your habits become your values, your values become your destiny."

In many important respects, I am not the same person I was as a youth, as a young adult, as a maturing, responsible family and working man, creating my usefulness and my story, built around self-absorption, career-seeking, dream-making for loved ones around me, and fighting and conquering addictive behaviors that when I felt deeply threatened, I let go of to save my self-worth. It was a serious business being responsible for the lives of others but I was gifted with some innate energy and optimism, in spite of certain shadowy and sabotaging thoughts that may have pursued me from time to time, and I was synchronistically blessed to have people pass into and through my life that were perfect for me at that moment and beyond.

Today I am participating in and celebrating the dreams of others around me; I have discovered a divine calling and the illumination of gifts within me, previously hidden, which now urges me to seek the youngest, the most vulnerable, the neediest, and the most worth celebrating—that is the children of the world outside my family who have become the heart and soul of me, of who I am, of who I have become.

Sometimes during our darkest nights of the soul, we slip most easily into giving up on others who need us, and generally not seeing the value of the gifts we have for others, and we block all ways and means to receive the good gifts and grace poised to work with us at the hour of our greatest need. It is in these moments that we are at the crossroad of consciousness, ready to summon beliefs, attitudes, change-agents, guidance from within . . . to bring us back to the reality of who we really are. For myself, I am grateful for my gifts of gentle fatherhood, light-hearted self-deprecating humor, the ability to meet others heart-to-heart, to celebrate their humanity, to be genuinely interested in the stories of their lives, so that I feel most alive in the company of others. I open myself in complete acceptance and appreciation for the gifts given to me of time, of the freedom to volunteer amongst the children who enter my life as blessings and as teachers, the gifts of friendship, wise counsel, spiritual way-showers and life coaches, and for my health to sustain me with energy and enthusiasm.

SEVERAL YEARS AGO, A BOOK DROPPED into my possession called *Three Cups of Tea*, written by Greg Mortensen, an expert mountain climber, who lost his way while traversing K2, the world's second highest mountain. He was found by a sherpa and taken to the sherpa's village in the remote region of Central Asia. During Mortensen's convalescence in the village, he noticed there was no school to educate the children, and particularly girls were excluded from what little education was being provided. His experience transformed him to become a humanitarian whose mission was to bring schools, especially for girls, to the region. After reading about Mortensen's work, a chord resonated in me to donate some money resources to his cause for advancing the educational opportunities, especially for girls, in that remote part of the world. To further support the needs of girls beyond our borders, we are financially sponsoring the education through college of a young lady in Mexico whose resources are limited but whose desire to achieve success for herself is apparent by her consistently high marks in high school and her eagerness to learn. I can see clearly now that I have been and will continue to look for ways to elevate the status of women through education.

There is a song that since I first heard it has haunted me each time I recall it. The song conjures up feelings of "how could that have happened," "wasn't there a way to resolve the differences?," "what a waste of lives and the potential for greater things . . . together." The song is "Say Something" by the group called A Great Big World. Here are some of the lyrics that tug at my heart:

"Say something, I'm giving up on you
I'll be the one if you want me to
anywhere I would've followed you . . .

And I am feeling so small
It was over my head
I know nothing at all . . .

And I will stumble and fall
I'm still learning to love
Just starting to crawl . . .

> *And I will swallow my pride*
> *You're the one that I love*
> *And I'm saying goodbye . . . "*

I am in this world to use all my strength, my resolve, my gifts, my compassion to serve those in most need of me, and I will never let my fears, foibles, impatience, or arrogance get in the way of my sacred service to others.

A new and exciting feeling comes over me as I am preparing to volunteer at our church's Sunday school . . . I am going to be meeting up with someone at the church; who that is to be and for what purpose I do not know. It is going to be spontaneous, serendipitous, and synchronistically arranged by an all-knowing and benevolently guiding universe. Arriving early to church before my assignment to volunteer, I sit at a vacant table in the community room, having coffee, and waiting for the next step. In my hands is an affirmation card inviting me to write something that focuses on what I want. This is what I write: "Today I am on a path to greater adventures, higher vistas, wider horizons, deeper illuminations of life's purpose, expanded usefulness, spontaneous and serendipitous connections leading to a higher calling to sacred service." I take it to an affirmation table, show it to a prayer practitioner who adds, "I am the answer to someone's question" and "I am open and receptive to new avenues to express my divinity." That day I found the stranger I was to meet and who was to join with me in completing the universe's current plan for my purposeful living.

CAN YOU BRING YOURSELF to believe the startling truth being played out in your life that what you are seeking, is seeking you; that the seeds you are planting in the garden of your hopes and dreams already know what they will become, if given the proper balance of sun, moisture, and length of growing season, mixed with your own unique, perhaps yet undiscovered, talents and gifts to do what only you can do, what only you have been called to do, at this time, in this place?

Would you like to believe that before you were born you had a prenatal conference with your Source where you were given a glimpse, a notion, a realization, an illumination, a sense of length, breadth, and depth of the physical life that was to be uniquely yours, and how the various twists and turns, meetings and leavings, comings and goings, successes and challenges, experiences and situations, personal growth and expansions of consciousness, revelations, miracles, spontaneities, synchronicities, serendipities and mind-changing encounters would leave you in awe and wonder with powerful teaching moments but also with undeniable four-square assuredness, and you said "amen" to it all; that your destiny would unfold as revealed, act its way out for the greatest good of all and that at any given moment in your life, you would be able to look back at the path you had walked, the forks in the road you had taken and would be able to see clearly now how events then came together as foretold and foreseen prior to your stepping on this Earth, to add multitudinous and abundant Good to the forces in the universe?

Should God grant me the grace of illumination to see my legacy even as I am in the midst of its unfoldment, I wish for it to be the image of softer days, full of celebration and praise, alive with useful pursuits, permeated with the laughter of little children, halos of hope around their heads, nothing to fear, safety always near, love and respect abiding and abounding . . . and years later when the sharp, clear images of each moment having fled from my memory, may there be an afterglow of gentle remembrance that still has the perfect power of intention, purpose ,and meaning to, even then, be useful to humanity.

It is a fundamental truth that what have been our experiences— in sum total and in sharp memory as significant individual events indelibly marked on our psyches—form patterns to create how we look and react to the world around us today. Perhaps for myself I am more guardedly optimistic and restrained from unbridled celebration when things are going really well in my life. My childhood years were a checkerboard of moves around the city of Chicago, occasionally requiring separation from one or the other parent for a short time, adjusting to new neighborhoods, schools, and carefully choosing just a very few close friends. I felt most at home in the institutional settings of school and church, which carried into my adult work life as my company being the hub of my social life as well. And now I am comfortably ensconced in the School of Life, participating, contributing, discovering my skills, thriving on participation in the lives of the smallest ones among us . . . seeing myself embedded in safe and secure, totally comfortable surroundings not always afforded me in my years growing up.

I speak my truth with clarity, joy, and love. I listen to that which speaks most strongly in me, waiting as student, as recipient, as gifted one wanting to give the world, plying my trade and my truth as I see it today, clarifying its continuous flow, immersing myself in the here and now, yet looking from the outside at the "me" in my present state, being the witness and the participant, interwoven in the fabric of my doing but willing also to extricate and remove myself from the allure and attraction of success and its applause, should intuition and the stirrings of my soul-self show me a different path, a new calling to be homaged and honored as my authentic self calling, and beckoning me to serve those most needy and vulnerable in my own unique way. As I ponder I continue to go about doing my right work, following my brightest stars, living my best life, in the present, not wedded to it but gleaning all good graces from it to be useful for the future me.

In my increasing awareness of powers within me that empower useful and compassionate altar calls of service to spring from me, to beckon me, to illuminate my path and foreshow my destiny . . . in this personal revelation of oneness and solidarity with all sentient beings, I give joy and life to all, knowing that the gift of life is not to me alone but to be revealed and shared, as I go about doing my right work, following my brightest stars, living my best life.

EACH OF US HAS A UNIQUE personal power, an energy, an intuitive source of potential for good that, when recognized and acted on, becomes a living, thriving source for right action that uplifts and supports all things everywhere that call for the presence of good to be demonstrated in our world. Feelings of lack or limitation, busyness, or not bothering to go deeper into one's soul-self obscure and hide our fundamental goodness and our gifts. Self-satisfaction and striving for what are promises to those who achieve the trappings of success as the world knows success, also are impediments to knowing and using our intangible but real gifts.

Thinking as and being a "child whisperer" was never in my game plan as a volunteer many years ago, but feeling that my gifts were usefully applied to the needs of children, acknowledged by knowledgeable professionals as impactful and valuable, has motivated me to continue on my path as sacred servant.

There is a poem by Rabindranath Tagore called "When I Grow Up." It speaks of the wistful nature of a child in the midst of their school day, seeing the world around them and envious of the adult activities they see through a child's eyes. The scene is perhaps a busy city in the Far Eastern part of the world. Walking to school, the child sees a Hawker, turbaned and bearded, sitting on a rug at street side calling out to those who pass by to buy the bracelets he made the night before. The child, in passing, muses how appealing this scene of the Hawker selling his wares looks and reflects on the freedom the child can only aspire to and must wait to grow up to feel the fruits of such a lifestyle. And after school, returning home the child sees a Gardener digging in a patch of soil, preparing the ground for seeding, planting, weeding, and watering. The child notices that the Gardener, in his work, has become hot, sweaty, and dirty, but in the child's mind's eye, there is no one who berates the Gardener for soiling his clothes and looking such a sight. The child in their world of need to follow proper behavior, including staying clean, neat, and tidy, wishes to be like the Gardener when they grow up, so no one will scold or call to account their disheveled or dirty appearance. And again at night, as the child looks out their bedroom window, a night watchman walks his beat and looks appealing as he stands under the streetlamp, able to stay up all night and do what he wants, the child again wishing to do as the watchman does but not able until they grow up . . .

I AM NOW ON THE BEACH, and if I should stop and canvass the crowd, converse with the older generation walking or lounging there, those who have, with the passage of time, been through the years of the child in the poem and are now reposing in the freedom of elder life, would they say it was all worth waiting for, that what they earned with their growing up was worth waiting for, the fruits of living what the child saw and was so wanting in the hawker, the gardener, and the watchman? Would they now declare a life fully lived or work yet to be done?

There is a group among our diverse population known by their extensive intelligence and their ability to recall facts and events from the past as if from a box of catalogued file cards. Their thoughts flow as their minds read each piece of information then blithely return it to the place from which it came—and then the next event or thought extracted to be examined, called forth, pondered, as if holding something precious in one's hand and turning it over and over. These are the people of the world who are the greatest among us in solving puzzles, jigsaw or crossword, sudoku and numbers . . . taking on and overpowering all such mind-bending games as these, undaunted, unflinching as in their mind's eye, they see the pieces and parts of the challenge before them as a wish fulfilled. And in so doing they once again satisfy the intellectual pursuits of their soul. And they go to places in the mind where only a few have ever been.

If a hero be thought of as being, above all, useful to others, to diligently spend a lifetime identifying individual gifts, honing them skillfully, seeking and not relenting until finding a way to put them into practice in the world, to be impactful and life-altering in ways that raise the self-worth and self-esteem of the neediest and most vulnerable of humanity; if all this is what a hero is, then I am that. If there never be accolades or tributes or triumphant processions marking loudly and laudably the part I, as hero, played in this game of life; if I leave this Earth without a ripple or a rumble of recognition other than to know that someone or some others have benefited at their core from my passing their way, my engaging their needs, my leaving them better for knowing the likes of me, I will rest in peaceful repose, better for having known thee and thou.

I know that aging is of human construct, designed to name, label, and pinpoint certain physical characteristics that end up by saying, "Sorry, but you have to accept your diminishment and prepare yourself in God's waiting room for your inevitable passing from this life, quietly and without a ripple of ever having been here or done much; at least you tried hard not to be a big bother at the end." I counter this cultural misapprehension, which misses the mark, and I joyfully affirm that I am aging as a sage with dignity, perfection and impactfully going about doing my own right work, following my brightest stars, living my best life.

I EMBRACE MY HUMOROUS essence as it wants to reach out and touch others, making their days a little brighter, a little more relational to the lighter side of life, a deeper connectivity to the less serious and more self-deprecating parts of our humanity, our foibles and our frivolities, our less serious side we wish to show more often to ward off the heaviness and demands of daily responsibilities droning on and insisting on being done . . . and in my heart I am saying, "Don't take me too seriously; I'm fun to be with; we can get through this together." I connect with joyous Spirit, our *Namaste* of nonsense, as I go about doing my right work, working the improv daily at the School of Life and elsewhere, following my brightest stars, living my best life.

I feel I am standing at a crossroads, at a fork in the road, with God standing forth in the world with me, knowing me best, and acting in divine concert with me as my destiny unfolds. It feels as if I am in midstream and must see this year's school volunteering to its calendar end. I just keep listening and learning, trusting my inner knowing to lead me, and looking for signposts and sentient beings to bring me guidance and purposeful thoughts that resonate with me. One thing is for sure and comes through clearly to me: I know and value my place in life, a life of usefulness and rich human connections, and in this knowing will direct and guide me through to my greater-yet-to-be.

Riding into a new adventure, but not beyond the back yard.

Standing straight and tall, eager to please, ready to serve.

My first paying job—grocery delivery boy with helpers, sister Pat and brother Bob.

The high school graduate.

Private First Class Roger T. Berg U.S. Army Finance Corp 1956-1959.

On military leave while serving in Europe; standing at the gate to the castle of Louis XIV in Versailles, France.

We're on hallowed ground as we teach and learn from the children in our midst.

Mom—first lady of our house and hearts.

The living legacy of this family
assures that the world going forward will be one that works for everyone.

Poised above the
Earth; to see
humanity below
him and the
sky above and
he knows
where God is.

I look outside our mountain home and see that winter
has left its gift of snow for us to enjoy throughout the Christmas holiday.

Mr. Copper, the hummingbird,
tries to keep everyone else
away from the bird feeder...
a daunting task, Mr. Copper,
and quite a greedy one.

We are here to love and protect the most
precious and vulnerable among us: our
children, animals, and all sentient beings.

I wish farewell to the setting sun
of another good day; I look forward
to the dawning of yet another day
of greater discoveries.

A quiet meadow opens before me and I give a blessing upon all humanity for a world reveling in natural beauty.

CHAPTER 6

Usefulness

Bringing Ultimate Meaning Into Our Lives

"Not all of us can do great things.
But we can do small things with great love."

"I alone cannot change the world, but I can cast a stone
across the waters to create many ripples."

— MOTHER TERESA

"Do your best to present yourself to God as one approved,
a worker rightly handling the word of truth."

— 2 TIMOTHY 2:15

i n t r o d u c t i o n

u   s   e   f   u   l   n   e   s   s

When I can gauge progress in the neediest and most vulnerable whom I have chosen to serve, children in the school setting, I feel eminently useful and meaningfully occupied, spurred on to remain all in, all the time, continuing to seek ways to serve others and ultimately make this a better world for all of us.

I walk quietly through the activities of my day, taking pleasure and joy in my usefulness for each task, celebrating my God-illumined gift of "child-whisperer" and knowing, gratefully, that I have found my calling, and it shows me its many faces in the children who come into my life.

It is in the stillness of these early morning hours that my appreciation and gratitude for my gifts open themselves to me, humble me in the immensity of their responsibility to show each soul their abilities and their self-worth, the joy of dilgence and determination, and the celebration of success. And in each people-encounter there is a moment of listening, of recognition, of stillness . . . when the connection is made, the door is open to receiving insights and personal messages Divinely delivered, Spirit-inspired, humanly acknowledged . . . taking the giver and receiver from glory to greater glory, from this beginning moving us forward to our greatest-yet-to-be.

My mantra and consistent and constant striving is that all things useful and life-giving come from my heart and manifest in my daily actions. In my mind's eye, I envision all that I have—time, talent, treasure, and personal energy—all of which are to be of sacred service to humanity, telescoped down to the people who enter my life, and in so entering and abiding awhile, leave with higher spirits, greater self-esteem, loftier goals and aspirations, deeper faith in their own abilities and power to walk through the world making a difference, and thus widening and expanding God's loving-kindness and boundless generosity of Spirit beyond me, beyond themselves, multiplying all the fruits of beneficence available, both materially and spiritually.

The rhythm and rhyme of each day sings a song that calls to me to get up, speak up, and begin moving into useful activities that by day's end have resulted in a betterment, a beautification of Spirit, an upliftment of some soul, an inspiration, a connection, a meeting of minds and hearts, an "Aha" moment or two, a laugh, an "oh my God," a discovery, a recovery, a hill climbed, a valley discovered, a person recognized and raised up, a life lived amidst the routine and flow of an ordinary life lived extraordinarily.

People, places, and perfect days all collaborate to create a continuous stream of supportive sacred service to fill my days with useful, unified activity and right action. I rejoice in my length of days, my vigor, my enthusiasm, my power of self-healing and healthy choices all coalescing into a life of oneness and wholeness with Spirit.

I SIT IN THE SERENITY of silent contemplation awaiting my next assignment; I work within the larger view and attraction to the highest calling of my soul-self, knowing that the details are all being worked out ahead of the daily toil, which shows up as my usefulness, the use of my gifts, my used-up energy at the end of the day, and knowing that I have given my all, imperfect and incomplete as that work may have been, to begin anew each day reaching higher realms of realizing my highest potential, my greatest good.

My imagination is the portal to higher realms of expanded spiritual living and doing for others. There is an incredible power in the universe, and I can use it if I so wish to access it as my divine rite of passage. First I must believe it, then I will see it.

It is most comforting and peacefully assuring to know that we do not have to work to satisfy some outside entity that judges our moves and our motives, that metes out justice and dictates right behavior for us to follow or else . . . but to know that "we embody within ourselves the whole Kingdom of God—infinity, not just a little bit of the kingdom, not just a small portion of God, but the Allness of God" (Joel S. Goldsmith). And so we come to know, little by little, as we look around at the wider world, as we walk among our brothers and sisters in faith, that our gifts become known to us, and we realize that we can use them to effect change in the world through our right action, all those things because we carry the Kingdom of God within, and "As our thought is opened and we behold the image of eternity within ourselves, we are changed by this image into a newness of life. This is accomplished by the Spirit of God" (*The Science of Mind*, Ernest Holmes, p. 489).

IF I HAD TOLD MYSELF when starting out nine or ten years ago that I would still be in the business of volunteering in schools, I would have been incredulous and probably in disbelief at such an idea. I was just coming off a long period of leisure and retirement living, filling in my days with golf, "fitness over 50" classes, and visiting family on long weekends and holidays . . . a nice rhythmic life of self-absorption, some writing and reading for self-improvement but certainly not conjuring up any challenges to my world of comfort and conformity as a senior citizen enjoying the fruits of my labors as a productive, working person.

Fast forward to now, and I am mentally preparing for my ninth year volunteering at school, going over in my mind the past experiences, my likes, loves, and not-so-goods, which took me from initial planning and expectations to outcomes and a final work product. Giving myself a "grade" is not as important as feeling that young lives have been impacted by my presence. I have a self-assurance that tells me I have been useful, and that surety brings me back for more.

CHAPTER 7

Intention & Purpose

Answering the Call To Be All that I Can Be

"Let us not be content to wait and see what will happen, but give us the determination to make the right things happen."

— PREACHER PETER MARSHALL

"Start by doing what's necessary, then what's possible, and suddenly you are doing the impossible."

— SAINT FRANCIS OF ASSISI

"A treasure rediscovered

A life redirected

A path uncovered

A purpose resurrected

A voice uplifted

An intention declared

A desire created

A world where all blessings are shared."

— ROGER T. BERG

i n t r o d u c t i o n

i n t e n t i o n   &   p u r p o s e

Sometimes in our youthful beginnings, we find ourselves stuck, suspended betwixt and between the insistently strong opinions of larger-than-life authority figures around us and our still developing, yet largely unformed and uninformed self-knowing, and we remain vulnerable to the whims and fancies of these self-proclaimed sages of all things important in life. We can only then proceed, reliant on Divine Intelligence and the speed of our intelligence gathering and experience building, our innate intuitive powers still developing, a sense of our authentic nature still growing, finding out what's right for us, all aspects of ourselves growing stronger within. We then proceed down life's path, armed and ready, gathering fruits and flowers of courage, illumination, epiphany moments of self-revelation, realizing the length and breadth of our gifts and talents to share, and picking up along the way the comfort and companionship of other genuinely caring friendship- and community-building souls, who are in it with us for the long haul.

*M*any songs sing in my heart, some harmoniously beautiful and filled with promise, peace, and hope for ever-better days of my life; other songs discordant and disturbing with crosscurrents of connection to the physical world of ego, striving, fear, lack, limitation, falling short, life ending with, "Have I done enough; could I have done more?"

I must continue to extricate myself from ideas and thoughts that keep me squarely in the "world of 10,000 things" and move through radical action and creative participation in the world of children, knowing that is my portal and my path to belonging to the universe in which I live, identifying my greatest good as one with Divine Intelligence, which is back of it all, guiding me.

No situation or circumstance can alter the trajectory of my path to my greater good. The power, the assurance, the certitude of my calling and my destiny is of God, and so I step aside and let God do its work in me. Without ego or concern for consequences or outcomes, I rest in God, which is within me, knowing that there are yet great things in store for me—that which I am called to do, that which I must do—yet to see manifestations of God's glory in all those who cross my path in mutual bonding and celebration of life.

I begin this day under the full head of steam of powerful intentions and high purpose. I let go of fear and grasp an attitude of positivity and enthusiastic anticipation of my plans succeeding, events unfolding in my favor, surprises supporting my every need, serendipity and synchronistic happenings combining to make this the best day ever.

I realize that I have a Power greater than myself that I can call upon to activate my thinking, my intelligence, my willpower, my purposeful and intentional radical action to read, to write, to reach out, to love, to effect positive change, to initiate insights and illumination and resolve, all for my advancement and God's greater glory.

Through me flows Divine purpose and right action, manifesting Godness and loving-kindness to all whose paths I cross, serendipitously and fortuitously, planned and delivered through Divine intervention and grace; I have eyes to see and ears to hear the plan of God in my life.

I FEEL THE NEWNESS AND EXPECTATION of new possibilities and expanded horizons of opportunity as I ride the exhilaration of the winter's first greeting of snow, its finest gift.

I keep myself awake and aware of any signs or signals that tell me to step in with compassion and understanding, with high resolve and purposefulness, so perfectly matched and meaningfully made to order for my gifts, talents, and resources, that each and every such encounter in time is resolved for the greater good of all.

From my smallness I reach for bigness, which is within me ready to ignite in radical action, torched and awakened by the realization that I am a difference-maker beyond my power to believe. And as I see events unfold, confirming my ability to hold service in all courts and conditions entrusted to me, I boldly go where I have never gone before.

Freedom is an inner feeling rising to the surface of my realization when I choose to know its truth in my life: When I believe it, I will see it, and freedom's fruits shall be made known to me as I let go of lack and limitation and seize my rightful heritage of God-given freedom.

A POWERFUL SOURCE OF MOTIVATION and intentional, purposeful living is the thoughts we allow to inhabit our mind and motivate our actions. If one can believe this and also believe that the universe stands ready to support us by responding to our words, our feelings, our thoughts, and our emotions in everyday situations, then we can embrace the powerful thought that changing our thinking, looking at things differently . . . can change our life. No more looking to forces and circumstances outside ourselves to find the reasons we are not living the life we were meant to live. It is in our power to change the course of our lives and to set sail for new, exciting shores of experience.

As Mahatma Ghandi instructed us: "Your beliefs become your thoughts, your thoughts become your words, your words become your actions, your actions become your habits, your habits become your values, your values become your destiny."

Caught up in the busyness and necessities of living daily, striving to find balance, quietude, usefulness, value, sometimes thriving, sometimes overwhelmed or being held hostage by shadow thoughts of "falling short" and "not being enough," somewhere in the mad melee of living, are our gifts waiting to be liberated and shared in the world, our light to be illuminated, our self-worth to soar, our reason to be becoming more clearly defined and delineated as people and events show up to give us clues, signs, and signals, insistent and persistent . . . that our special gifts are needed, our calling must be heeded, our past life of slumber and sleeping with our gifts not repeated. It is perhaps a series of small, unobtrusive, unnoticed encounters carrying deeper meaning than first realized. Pray to be awake and aware of these promptings of Spirit as they pass in and out of your life. They themselves are gifts, seeking to divinely inspire us to see farther, climb higher, reach further, live deeper, create magnificently a life worth living.

For me, generating feelings of gratitude on a regular basis creates the opening and the invitation to appreciate the abundant life all around me. When, on the other hand, my striving for more takes the focus off what I already have and puts me in the grip and lock of lack and limitation, I find myself striving but never arriving. An anonymous source asks a challenging question: "If we do not feel grateful for what we already have, what makes us think we'd be happy with more?"

Ernest Holmes delivers this message to us: "God wills us to have everything. As we express life, we fulfill God's law of abundance, but we do this only as we realize that there is good enough to go around— only as we know that all of God's gifts are given freely and fully as the air and the sunshine . . . alike to all."

I will keep firmly and affirmatively as my right intention to see the act of gratitude as the portal through which I step to give a joyous response to the beauty and beneficence of life, as I go about doing my right work, following my brightest stars, living my best life, abundantly enriched, and blessedly fulfilled.

PURPOSEFUL LIVING offers the best chance that we will live life to its fullest, that we'll have recognized and responded to the needs of every significant other, every casual passerby, every opportunity to serve, every chance for personal growth, to see things differently, to stretch beyond the pale of our limited experiences, to see inside the soul of another, to walk in their shoes, to absorb their pain, to be brother to all other brothers and sisters within our reach and our calling. There is a corner of this world to which we have been transported to do meaningful work, to model the best in ourselves, to be strong, to shore up others where they are weakest, to celebrate the overcoming of physical infirmities, of debilitating disease when the road of life looks too short for the youngest amongst us. We are blessed and honored to walk the walk among the sentient beings whom we have found on our path, and in someone else's concern and need we have found our purpose.

To plan, to conceptualize, to set out in great detail, to visualize, to be attached to outcome is how we set objectives for ourselves and how we expect the greatest results of our desires to be achieved. Of course, life never turns out exactly as we have envisioned it; sometimes we are pleasantly surprised but more times than not, the unfolding of reality brings some elements of disappointment with it. Reality just has not fit neatly into our rigid picture of how things should be . . . again. There is another way . . . a surrendering of outcomes and results, a turning over to higher powers, to greater intelligence in the universe, to the God within us who knows our needs, to the guidance of bringing the most good to the highest number of the neediest among us; that is the highest purpose that dwells above our vision boards, our detailed planning, our fences placed around what we should feel . . . what sets us free to appreciate, anticipate, celebrate the unknown but knowable coming our way.

Going offline, making space and distance between you and daily, familiar, demanding life . . . to a beach paradise, having a different rhythm and flow than your daily comings and goings, an opening up to new perspectives of what could be and what you could yet become . . . is like flying above the Earth at 30,000 feet, seeing the landscapes, the cloud formations, the broad and wide vistas of valleys and hills, mountains and molehills, cities teeming with folks, rural scenes of farms and fertile pastures . . . and from your higher realm of illumination and free-spirited thought, you open yourself to new possibilities, greater awareness of work to be done, seeing more potential for the use of your abilities and talents, and as we come back to our Earth-bound existence, opportunities previously hidden in plain sight begin to emerge and play insistently upon our thoughts, forming ideas and plans to be useful, to serve higher purposes, to serve and save the world . . . and we realize we have returned from paradise and we are back in the Game of Life.

CHAPTER 8

School of Life

A Special Place of Being and Becoming

"You teach best what you most need to learn."

—RICHARD BACH

"That is what learning is.

You suddenly understand something you've understood

all your life, but in a new way."

— DORIS LESSING

s c h o o l   o f   l i f e

The School of Life is, at first glance, an edifice of educational endeavor, a building of brick and mortar, corridors, classrooms, and common areas, animated and energized with the various activities to engage our youngest in the teaching and learning process, arming them with the necessities of knowledge, equipping all as lifelong learners to traverse and sustain themselves in the wider world outside home and hearth. Beneath the surface of busyness, there is at work the natural process of people engaging each other at the human level where respect, inclusion, diversity, safe passage, and all elements of basic human rights and values are safeguarded, celebrated, and encouraged to flourish and to be enjoyed, equally and unequivocally, by all who pass through the doors of this School of Life.

I listen and I learn from all my spiritual teachers and way-showers: from family, my teachers, and the kindred spirits coming to me as the children at school—sometimes the little ones teach me and sometimes I teach them—it is a mutual give-and-take, and in the process, I grow as a teacher and embody sacred spiritual principles by practicing empathy, patience, celebration, and, yes, sometimes, tough love. I stand in the midst of a life of spiritual revolution, which only grows me and moves me to higher realms, to expanded living the life I am called to live.

In my volunteer teaching experience, I have become more thoughtful, circumspect, humble, patient, empathetic, creative, celebratory, awestruck, grateful, positive, fair, forthright, confident, and definitely living the dynamics of my teaching/learning experience—so my words have been multiplied in their power and range of impact, bringing back to me the immense responsibility when I stand before the world of my young charges and present myself as "teacher."

Using up energy to fight our internal demons can never have a good outcome. Seeing things differently, asking ten questions that start with "what if . . . " can set our mind in a direction that puts us back in balance, adds perspective to our lives, and may even set us off in radical resolve and action, bringing positive results to ourselves and to others. Having infinite patience with our circumstances will bring the universe into play to assist us, with the most amazing results.

I find this happening in the classroom when I am dealing with people who are easily distracted, disruptive to others, and who I know have the intelligence to learn, but who are self-destructing before my very eyes. Things go more smoothly when I show patience and empathy with them, but I still wonder sometimes if I could get them to concentrate more if I took a heavier hand with them. . . . It is the universal dilemma facing all teachers of younger, K-8 students.

Going within to find stillness does not always mean hiding out in solitude and safety away from the cares of the world to catch one's breath. Sometimes it is standing in the midst of chaos and confusion, arming yourself with patience and a compassionate heart, seeing beyond the moment, taking ego out of the picture, staying the course . . . where the true work of God can be done. . . . I am sorely tested sometimes in classrooms by the little band of recalcitrant students, unwilling or unable for a variety of reasons to follow directions, pay attention, or stop being major distractions to each other during class.

So the enlightenment here is that I can only control my own behavior and stifle any judgmental emotions that may try to seep in and destroy whatever value can be gleaned from the situation. It is for me to provide the framework and the fertile ground wherein the souls entrusted to me can grow at whatever pace it is in their capability to do so, in spite of any outer manifestations to the contrary.

That which I am now doing, what I have come to know is my destiny and my calling . . . to be a volunteer in schools and to always be in the presence of children as my main passion for the rest of my life

. . . has only come slowly to me, illuminating my path over the last eight or nine years. My passion for what I am and what I do with children has been like a slow, low flame of wanting to be useful and wanting to continue to learn what essentially was a new craft, a new skill . . . and the teaching and learning environment ignited my interest and touched my heart. To be among the most dedicated and intelligent people in their field, to watch teachers skillfully manage their classrooms, and to be among the most vulnerable and needy of humanity . . . our children . . . became, to my enlightened mind, an honor and a privilege. I entered the door of the School of Learning and found through the years that it really is the School of Life, where we all learn to care about each other as we find out who we are becoming in the world.

WHEN I STARTED VOLUNTEERING nine years ago in Rancho Mirage, California, I walked into the classroom having constructed a certain notion of what I had to offer, bundled tightly inside me, with its boundaries, its limits, its defined yet generalized desire to be of service and useful in some capacity dealing with children. I had no idea that the dynamics of interacting with teachers in their classrooms or the varieties of children's personalities, their backgrounds, just the free spirits and totally spontaneous beings that they were would combine to steal my heart away and allow me to surrender some of my rigidity and focus on being attached to my performance in the classroom and just enter into the magic and the delight of being a part of the teaching and learning dynamics. I started it all with certain expectations, limited by what I thought I had to offer, and as I gained courage and insight, going deeper into the process, making myself more vulnerable and available to my emerging gifts, I received far more than I ever imagined.

It seems that when we say "yes" to a new opportunity, it leads to so many other "yeses." Our view of what is coming next may be limited, narrow, and focused on the immediate task at hand, but out there beyond our present knowing may lie ever-growing and expanding possibilities and the potential to serve a larger purpose. I was led to volunteer in a school setting, quite content and actually adamant about wanting to confine my activities to the lowest levels of elementary school. My view of my role was to follow the directions of the teacher and not go outside the parameters of what I thought I could do.

Over the last nine years of volunteering, working with a dozen or more teachers in classrooms, both elementary and middle school, my scope and reach of activities have included teaching Junior Great Books to first and second graders, mentoring students on an individual basis, and acting as a male role model in the upper grades where there are fewer volunteers. I am humbled and honored, knowing the weight of responsibility I have accepted in being a part of the teaching and learning experience in what I call the School of Life.

I AM STRUCK WITH WONDERMENT and awe at the evolution of my life from a corporate business person, honing my professional skills in finance, accounting, cash management, and the like, to immersing myself in the School of Life, being in the presence of children, standing in the flow of youthful energy, participating in the miracle of the teaching/learning process, affecting and being affected by dedicated school administrators and teachers, and remaining humble and grateful for it all. There is a power that runs through this School of Life, and it carries meaningful lessons and messages to be learned and heeded. Not all teaching goes one way —from adult to child. I am struck with the realization that we are all so dedicated to creating life experiences for our children that enhance and celebrate their uniquenesses, their energies, their playfulness, their worth and value to themselves . . . I have come to see also their vulnerabilities and their fragility . . . which fires me up to be ever watchful to protect their safety and security.

Oh Lord, it is hard to be humble when situations arise, and they are many, when I know I am right and others are wrong. How can we come together and stay together as God's people if we have not humbled ourselves before each other and acknowledged our unworthiness —and showed our willingness to be of sacred service among our people? Particularly for me, when my teaching authority and superiority is challenged, and legitimately so, I back up only so far and then I play the "I am in charge" card to reassert my authority. No one really wins in these situations.

A far better story and result came when I was working with two math whizzes, second graders who clearly knew how to solve a particular problem. As they worked away, I acknowledged "I didn't know" and asked them to explain it to me when they were done. At the end, when I said to them that their work had gotten to the point where I understood, they felt pride in their accomplishment, particularly in showing their "teacher" the answer, and in the end we felt more collaborative than teacher-student. Their self-worth and esteem got a major boost that day.

My volunteer experience in the School of Life, which was carried on behind the walls and the brick and mortar of real elementary and middle schools, has taken a path, illuminating and instructive, from a personal image of teaching and imparting knowledge to students, like a mother bird feeding her young, to seeing myself in much more collaborative and joint-learning experience with my students. It has become a much freer exchange, a more authentic relationship, a growing in appreciation of the dynamics of teaching and learning, a common ground that fosters humbleness and compassion in the process, without the need or the desire to hold myself to such high standards of excellence that there is no room for living large in the School of Life.

I have come a long way from that day in my first year of volunteering, when a middle school boy, confused at seeing me in his classroom for the first time asked, "Are you an ordinary teacher?" My rather impulsive and naïve reply was, "No, I am an extraordinary volunteer." So began that day for me the humbling and dismantling of the perfect teacher image.

The concept of vulnerability has entered my life in multiple ways, showing up in myriad places as my teacher and my way-shower, as my light illuminating parts of me previously hidden and undiscovered, and deepening my compassion and my call to serve those most vulnerable and needy in the wider world around me. My personal path of vulnerability showed up in me at an early age as wanting to be a good son, to be useful, non-demanding, to live up to my self-imposed expectations of what would make my parents happy and proud of me. I judged myself to have done a good job in being the proper son in a family that I discovered later, on reflection, was struggling with their own life stories.

Today my current calling, my primary reason to be, has drawn me to the School of Life, wherein I have discovered and been strongly drawn to the vulnerability of the children I have come to care about in ways that have expanded and created places in my heart I never knew I had. I am in awe of the miraculous gift of "child-whispering" I have discovered in me, of the ultimate connection of adult-soul to child-soul, honoring the joining of our spiritual selves to each other.

I am in awe, humbled, and in high gratitude when I contemplate and reflect on my teaching and learning experiences in what I call the School of Life. The classrooms in which I spend my days, this late in my life, when the moments of my living seem more precious and dear to me as they tick away into an ever shortening future . . . these class-rooms hold students and teachers whom I call "my family," just as real and commanding my loyalties and my energies as my family of blood and birth. Each day in this School of Life I walk among my brothers and sisters who are dedicated and devoted to the most needy and most vulnerable among us, our children, preserving, expanding, enthusing the minds of our youngest ones, to send them on as seeds to grow into trees we will never sit under but which we were a party to creating.

DID YOU EVER THINK of yourself as a superb storyteller or a dream-weaver? Most of us love to hear good stories, and it all starts at a very young age when we go to the library, sit on the rug, and listen to a granny-type read a book to us and intersperse anecdotes and embellishments to bring the stories alive. Our young minds were taken deep into the world of flight and fancy, where dragons roamed and princesses found princes who were to their liking. Star Wars and Minecraft have invaded the mind-space of children, mostly the boys, to bring a huge techno-logical boost to their imaginations.

As we all grow up, our stories become more practical, more strictly planned out, more goal and success oriented. They lose their childhood innocence and playfulness. I suppose that is why I hang around the halls and classrooms of schools, to capture, perhaps for the first time in my life, the carefree and imaginative spirit of children learning and at play, unencumbered by the duties and obligations of managing life's responsibilities. . . . It is a good place to be, dwelling in the Land of Lollipops and Dragons.

I have come to know my essential self, my deepest and most authentic self, by seeing myself unfold and respond to situations in the classroom. I am essentially a peace-maker and a child-whisperer around the children I work with. Occasionally I am taken advantage of, but then I either overcome the bad behavior of a student by finding and appealing to their sense of fairness with me, or bringing into the situation a connection to what interests them. If all else fails, I come down on them with genuine anger and frustration, and then they know the game they are playing has come to an end. I enjoy it most when I can find what motivates a student, what interests them, what takes them out of their sleepy disinterestedness and animates and excites them to tell me more or show me what they can do. It is when I can activate the spark within them to learn by my encouragement and showing them that they are worthwhile, perhaps they are not getting much encouragement and praise elsewhere in their young lives and we are here to shore them up.

As the school year nears its end, after 800 hours of volunteering in classrooms, mentoring students on a one-to-one basis—who need guidance in planning, organizing, focusing—and teaching Junior Great Books to first and second graders, the thought starts to bubble up in my brain, "What do I want to be doing at the school next year?" Early on, eight years ago when I started, my driving desire was to repeat the previous year's experience, pretty much exactly as it was before, and to keep my day filled with activities with no downtime while I was in the school building. I filled the summers with tutoring kids in their homes, and I was thrilled to do it.

Today my efforts are just as effective and impactful but with less of a feeling of intensity and being driven. My approach is softer, more deeply driven to find the place inside the student, that still point that sparks their interest and motivates their minds to say, "This is me. This is what I am. This is what I feel. This is what I care about!" And I am privileged and blessed to accompany these "big souls with short legs" on their journey of self-discovery and having fun as they go.

LOOKING BACK, MANY YEARS AGO I had a minimalistic and quite manageable view of what my role as a school volunteer would be. It was neatly wrapped and defined as wanting to be useful and helpful in the classroom, as much directed to assisting the teacher as working with the children. Initially, I felt some risk in thinking that my presence in the classroom could have any profound effect on the children in their learning process. Over time I began to stretch my thinking as to the impact I wished to make and began to realize that I could get inside the heads of these little ones, engage them at their level of how they viewed the world, imbue them with responsibility for their own behavior in the learning process, and celebrate and praise them when they were successful.

I moved from having limited goals to discovering my gifts as a child whisperer, acknowledging that I, too, was learning and that when I, the student, was ready, the teacher appeared, in many forms, in many places, through many people. I opened myself to taking risks and my growth as a teacher has been immense—by leaps and bounds.

I have enjoyed listening, many times over, to the song by One Direction called "The Story of My Life." The video is touching and unique as it flashes back to scenes of each singer's family, portraits and pictures that are placed affectionately on mantels in parlors and high places in their homes. Current pictures of the families are also interspersed throughout the video.

Next week in front of a group of second graders I will be telling the story of my life as part of a writing exercise in which they will be telling the world their stories in a memoir format. Besides telling them the facts of my birth, places I've been, people who have come and gone in my life, life-altering experiences, and so on, it seems to me the most impactful time in my life is the present moment, the here and now. As I look out on the sea of second-grade faces, I am struck by the fact that I have a unique connection with each one. I've met their parents and grandparents, shared stories, worked hard on assignments with them, celebrated their successes . . . so my story will be immediate and alive in the present moment, the best time of all . . . the here and now.

LAST YEAR I ATTENDED AN EVENT at Mile Hi Church, featuring the renowned metaphysical thought-leader as speaker, Deepak Chopra. Among other things, he shared the exercise that on a nightly basis, before going to sleep, one should do a recapitulation of the day's events, leaving out any judgment or falling short, but drift into sleep with positivity and satisfaction as your last thoughts. It has not always been easy to find a day's silver linings or spectacularly successful moments, when I focused on my efforts at school. Sometimes, the kids just get in the way of me being that "sage on stage" as a great teacher dispensing knowledge to the needy or so I thought. My feelings of connecting with students at their deepest level of interest and awareness would show up when I brought the greatest amount of empathy and patience, willing to meet them where they were on that day, not try to fit them into some pre-planned image of outcome or results. My days, in those epiphany moments, became lighter to carry, my self-satisfying demeanor rebounded, I felt useful and worthy to be "teacher," and my Deepak-motivated nightly recapitulations became success stories.

There can be no jealousy, no animosity, no prejudicial behavior, no lack or limitation, no withholding of resources, no personal roadblocks of worry and self-concern carried around in oneself creating inefficiencies or distractions . . . none of these things can be happening if the functions of teaching and learning are to enjoy their greatest success in the classrooms, behind the walls of the School of Life, initiated by the best in our teachers, received efficiently and effectively, creatively, enthusiastically, with lasting impact to be carried by students into their futures, constructing a world that works for everyone. No teacher can carry the weight of their own personal world into the classroom without adversely affecting the flow of learning, the give and take of teaching, the epiphany moments, the enlightened understanding when struggles become triumphs, self is celebrated and praised, raised to the highest levels of self-satisfaction and accomplishment. Yes, this is a heavy responsibility pressed upon teachers—to perform at their best in spite of their own human foibles and shortcomings. Their self-sacrifice is not too high a price to pay.

It seems we run across moments and opportunities for reflection in the strangest places, and when we act on their enlightened message, we are participating in some kind of magical exchange with the universe working on our behalf. In sixth grade Language Arts class where I volunteer, students read the poem by Shakespeare from *Hamlet* in which Hamlet ponders his fate, wonders what he should do. The monologue starts out, "To be or not to be. That is the question." I myself seem to be at the crossroad of opportunity with thoughts of new beginnings tugging at my sleeve: "To volunteer or not to volunteer"—whether it is better to advance the understanding and learning of other human beings or to use the preciousness of such time for personal improvements, leisure activities, or just any frivolous, free pursuits that pleasure me.

Ah, to assist the most vulnerable and neediest among us is indeed the highest calling, the deepest meaning of self-sacrifice; to have great learning opportunities as teacher is gift to me. On the other hand, to rob myself of personal time, creativity, time to recreate at leisure. Ah, the ticking of the clock, moments more precious in my older age than when following youthful pursuits. How to be or not to be . . . that is the question.

I FIND THAT THE CHANGING FACE of nature as seasons come and go, the school calendar marking the trimesters for grading and the September openings and May closings, holidays and birthdays, remembrances of loved ones who have transitioned to their greater glory causing us to stop and reflect at their passing . . . all of these and more have come to serve me as I reflect on my own passage of time and ask the pointed, direct question to self: Am I positioned in the very best place, mentally and physically, to act out the dictates of my heart, to lavish and indulge my gifts on those people most in need of me, all of my skills, my strength, my soul-self turned loose to do all the good I am called on to uncover and proffer and produce?

So now, as school is again winding up and winding down, the summer looms ahead to serve as a respite place for strength gathering and soul searching. Who do I want to be in the new school year, for there most certainly will be another school year for me. I will be guided in ways that provide a foundation, an infrastructure of familiar activities with ample space for Spirit to enter in and guide me to deeper, new experiences in the School of Life.

Almost nine years ago, unbeknownst to me, I was standing at the foot of a mountain of opportunity for service to others that was going to take me on a life-transforming, exhilarating, powerfully motivating journey into dozens of classrooms, over thousands of hours, interacting with hundreds of students and teachers, raising my level of awareness that in myself was the intent to sacredly serve, humbly give of my gifts, and have myself prosper personally in so many unimaginable ways, just by me saying "yes" and letting the power of intention go out to the universe to take me where I was most needed. It all started as a rejection of sorts from a children's hospital, which said that no help was needed in their reception area at this time. It led me to seek out other avenues and chances to serve children, landing me in pre-K, elementary, and middle school classrooms in three schools, teaching to classes of kids, as well as mentoring students with special abilities and special needs.

I have come full circle from eight years ago by now entertaining the idea of offering art activities and other fun things to children in local hospitals this summer. The intention is out there; I am now awaiting further instructions from Spirit.

WHEN EXPECTATIONS ARE OUTRUN by reality, giving us diminished or not looked for outcomes, our first go-to place of emotional response may be disappointment, unhappiness, and a feeling that again "I deserve what I get, because that is all my smallness of self can expect to happen." In some small part of ourselves there is a place stored with disappointments and failed expectations that are ready to spring forth when outer conditions and situations line up in a way that we are reminded of past dark times and falling short.

In schools, I have seen student behaviors and language that tell me that just below the surface of their daily lives lies grieving for things lost, people gone from their lives, mistakes made, choices not in their own self-interest acted on . . . constant reminders of loss, falling short, not good enough . . . which establishes a pattern of negative emotional responses on a daily basis. Those of us who remain awake and aware of these situations can model positivity and hope to these vulnerable ones, raising them up and celebrating the specialness of their personhood.

This week it has been demonstrated to me that "as you think, so goes your life." All year long I have had a love-hate relationship with one class where I volunteer. I love the subject matter and the way the teacher presents the material, with personal passion and enthusiasm, but there are days I want to hurry out of there at the end of class because I feel some of the kids wasted and squandered precious moments, self-destructing in the desire to entertain each other and look good in the eyes of classmates they wish to impress. It may be typical at that age, but it is a recipe for disaster for some because they don't have the internal resources to waste time . . . they need the help and wish to wave it off for gaining applause from their peers.

RECENTLY I HAD A TRANSFORMATION, gave myself a talking to, and decided to care about each of these souls, show patience in my dealings with them, and treat them as a servant leader should, acknowledging their worth and encouraging them. I choose to find in each person their sticking points, their hot buttons, their happy places, their tickle spots; for you see, I wish to be transformed into a force for good.

As we settle nicely into a comfortable daily routine, that is the time we experience nudges of . . . "Is this all there is?" or "I know I have inside more to give, but what and to whom?" or "If not me, who; if not now, when?" Amidst the opulent, recreational lifestyle of seven months in Sun City, California, urgings and callings to evolve into a newer state of conscious being, more humanitarian, more unselfish, more giving of my gifts, was awakening in me. Against the backdrop of having it all, living large in retirement and leisure, I slowly—without knowing the outcome but sure of the path in front of me—took the plunge into the world of lower elementary school dynamics, which was for me to become The School of Life. There I would meet not only teaching and learning but social interactions, teacher to students, students to students, and those of our most needy and vulnerable struggling to make sense of themselves and their world without sufficient adult modeling in their life to guide them at home or anywhere other than by adults in the classroom. This is where I found inside myself love, compassion, a genuine caring, and joy to give to all those I meet on my path.

Being a philanthropist has many faces and shows up in action in all sorts of places. It's not just money to spend on the needy and wanting; it is also knowing your gifts and being in sacred service in their using. Being and doing for others is the best life to live; giving yourself away is the best way to give. . . . In my younger days I focused on wanting to be a philanthropist, visibly atop a major dispensing machine-like operation, deciding who gets what and researching the best bang for our charitable buck. As time went on, no lottery jackpot fell into my hands to enable me to dole out monies to grateful masses.

However, running parallel with this self-centered dream, I was toiling and learning how to find my gifts and use them quietly and impactfully in The School of Life. I sit in front of a sea of upturned faces; they tell me what it has meant for me to come into their lives and help them spell, rhyme their poems, find their own stories. And I have not spent one dime on them, other than giving of myself totally and freely, doing what I love to do in sacred service and love.

THERE IS A QUOTE ATTRIBUTED TO THE SUFI MASTER, Rumi, that has haunted my reverie from time to time in various contexts and circumstances. . . . In my mind's eye today I am gathering children around me. . . . They are exuberant, trying to please and impress with their energetic shouts and laughter, pushing and jostling, excited for what's next, where are we going, knowing it will be full of fantasy and adventure. And into this picture of adolescent exuberance steps Rumi: "Out beyond ideas of wrongdoing and rightdoing there is a field. I'll meet you there." . . . And so we all gather in the field of expectancy and surprises, things not yet known but discoverable through the magic of teaching and learning . . . and I, the adult among the innocence of children, gets to play the part of the child once more, my youth gone but recaptured in this moment in time, and I get to relive it over and over again even though age and retreating mind-set and fleeting consciousness try to leave me. I can remain a child among children, whomever I become.

Behind the door marked Child Whisperer, there is a land populated and peopled by fantastically fanciful characters who are known by the names of Alice (as in Wonderland), Winnie the Pooh, Dr. Suess, Dorothy (as in the Land of Oz) and the like . . . roaming around randomly in the imaginative, creative minds of children of all sizes and ages . . . and how have I come to be and to feel I am that child whisperer? In some magical, magnificent, extraordinary stroke of serendipity and synchronicity, my gifts and my circumstances coalesced and combined to deliver me to the doorstep of the School of Life, wherein the children were waiting to lead me and teach me the ways of seeing life differently . . . through the eyes of children, showing me my innate child skills . . . and so I am enabled and armed with creativity, imagination, gifts, and skills newly found, dormant and now demonstrating the ability to connect on many levels of childlike delight and fancy—and in so doing, reach the children beyond fantasy and fairy tales to math, writing, reading, and the tools for their future.

Looking over the sea of upturned faces in the classroom as the teacher models the lesson for the day, a whole stream of dynamic behavior is being acted out, and in a first grade environment the challenges of teaching and learning can test the mettle and determination of even the most experienced professionals. Yes, this is the School of Life, where social skills and responsible behavior go right along with reading, writing, and 'rithmetic. Here kids are taught the skills of "whole body listening," being attentive, cooperative, learning to be responsible and certainly not trying to entertain one's neighbor while the teacher is talking. Smooth, quiet transition between activities is a goal seldom reached; easily picking up after oneself leads to a neat and tidy classroom; and, of course, helping any friend in need is paramount.

For myself, I find it easy to praise and say "thank you" to any student who is going in the right direction with their actions. These are magical moments when you see breakthroughs in behavior or eyes light up when tough things are learned, and you celebrate with a student their successes in learning. It is a joy to be in the midst of this school dynamic where gratitude abounds.

THERE IS NO OTHER PLACE in the universe like the classroom, full of energetic young souls with short legs engaged with the adult world, led by enthusiastic, driven-to-achieve, high-expectancy teachers, ever optimistic and always betting that at the end of the day, knowledge and love of learning will win out over any roadblocks and cultural conditioning trying to resist the march of personal empowerment taught in the School of Life. I have come to realize that my own motivating force and energy to be a part of this scene stems from two questions implicitly asked of the teachers whom I serve: What do you wish to accomplish? and How may I help you with it? My partnering with teachers in the classrooms becomes useful and impactful as I see us reaching further, delving more deeply, providing needed attention, discovering and addressing issues, averting disasters, providing security and safety, patching up differences, celebrating successes, seeing breakthroughs, smiling often, laughing loudly, commiserating, communicating, evaluating, and at the end of the school year, sending students onward, some with trepidation, but to all the hope that what was given them here in the classroom will serve them well.

Contained within the brick and mortar walls of the structure of teaching and learning called PreK-8 elementary/middle school, there is another reality of energy and action pulsating through the hallways and corridors generated by the occupants within, which I choose to call The School of Life. It lives and breathes a life of its own below the surface of what one can see objectively. I am humbled and respectful of the importance and sheer magnitude of the social dynamics of behavior and mental life that abound beneath the surface of daily classroom schedules and activities.

This hidden reality has insistently and forcefully challenged me to prepare as best I can to meet the daily challenges of school, to model my own best behavior, to prepare both physically and mentally to be the best I can be as I offer my gifts, to have patience and withhold judgment in all situations, to create an atmosphere of awe and wonder in the process of discovery and learning, to have high expectations for students' success, but to always be mindful that outside the world of school, everyone is dealing with personal matters of family, self and the wider world. . . . So being a safe harbor for others is also needed.

If I told you that on a regular basis I have heard a youngster repeat out loud, "This is the worst day of my life," and another one yelling loudly to no one in particular, "I am not worth anything," or words to that effect, and then see them many times act out this self-deprecation by annoying behavior with their peers, would that disturb you, move you to have remorse and compassion for these youngsters, make you want to reach out and enfold them in reassuring words and gestures that they are totally and completely loved of God and they are worthwhile and of the highest value as human beings in spite of their fears and frustrations with themselves to the contrary? This is what I see and hear occasionally in the School of Life, an acting out among our precious, most vulnerable beings, their feelings of lack and limitation in themselves. Their calling out for help or recognition is not always overt and dramatic, but it is there underpinning their thoughts and words and actions. If I can intervene, facilitate raising them up, getting them out of their funk, I mean to do so.

EARLY IN MY NEW LIFE as "one who serves children in the useful capacity as school volunteer," I had a limited but for me an appropriate plan to confine myself to dispensing knowledge to students in strict accordance with instructions from the teacher. No need to deviate since the teacher was the final word on how the teaching and learning process was going to go forward. I still, today, work within the teacher's guidelines and what motivates me to follow their guidance is a strong desire to learn teaching methods, practices of classroom discipline, how students are kept engaged, and to be a part of what I see as magical moments, "Aha" moments, when students are "getting it" and the teacher is genuinely pleased and happy, celebratory, and praising the efforts of their students.

As time has progressed, eight years, I have also progressed in taking on a more independent teaching role as I have gained the confidence of the teachers and, discovering more of my own abilities, encouraged myself to take on a larger teaching role, gone deeper into my volunteer experience, finding my gifts of showing, relating to, creating with, and inspiring children.

There is an art and a fine balance between teaching children specific social skills and knowledge that will be useful throughout their lives, all in the context of the classroom setting . . . and as the teacher, relating to each student in the deepest and most effective way for them individually, while at the same time acknowledging and coping with the diversity of family backgrounds, mental capacities, physical abilities, personality expressions, and one's own energy level and capacity to assimilate and deliver a "learning" product that teaches the best results. "One size does not fit all" is certainly the overriding theme in the School of Life. I am most enthusiastic and at my best as a child whisperer in the lower elementary grades, as I slip most easily into meeting the children on their own terms, being absorbed into their world of reality, where laughing and crying come easily, where they wear their emotions on their sleeves, and where they are in awe of the adult world all around them. My most satisfying moments are to be welcomed into their world as one of them, not as an adult.

When students are in their "passing period" in middle school, that three-minute drill to get from one classroom to the next, changing subjects, changing rooms, new teacher . . . some degree of responsible behavior is needed to accomplish this movement and then to settle down in a different environment and be ready to work. This is not like a well-choreographed play even though it is rehearsed day after day throughout the school year. When the bell rings to start class, some students haven't settled down, still talking about this or that with friends; some, having discovered their entertainment value, are encouraged by their peers to continue to perform long after class has started. These are the ones, distracting a distraught teacher, who are deposited in the back of the room where I am ready to rein them in and bring them back to focused behavior. Teaching the love of learning where I am sitting can be a challenge, but my little band of recalcitrants have taught me to show patience, to look beyond the obvious, to go deeper, to try harder myself to reach these young minds without alienating them but still modeling for them a better way to a bigger payoff in life.

WHEN DID I COME TO KNOW that I wanted to spend the rest of my natural life with and around children, in a school setting where the magic of teaching and learning was the driving energy force? Perhaps it was in the early days working with my grandchildren, creating with them stories and imaginings by starting with no plan and going to wherever our made-up thoughts would take us. Drawing and writing, thinking and discussing, drawing us into worlds of fantasy, unusual character connections, and using what was in front of us to make a most fanciful and entertaining world of our own. This idea of creating something out of nothing, using only one's imagination, experiences, and the unlikely connection of characters and plots coming seemingly from out of nowhere, came to be the driving force and the delight of my life. And I found that innate drive for self-actualization when I was among the children and teachers in the School of Life, who welcomed me in and have allowed me to do the work I love to do, to follow my brightest stars, to live my best life.

Today in my readings I came across thoughts that struck me as profound and gave me pause to think more deeply about my place in the scheme of things, in the longer view of seeing life move to me, through me, and carry on after me, not the same for having met me. From Elton Trueblood: "A man has made at least a start on discovering the meaning of human life when he plants shade trees under which he knows full well he will never sit." And from a Zen proverb: "The seed planted never sees the flower in its blooming."

In my years of volunteering at the School of Life, I have been in teaching and learning situations with hundreds of children from elementary school into middle school. I have had the privilege and been struck by the immensity of the experience to work with students in sixth grade that I first worked with in first grade—some of them in more than one grade as they proceeded through their schooling. Even with this unique and rewarding experience for me, there is always the time when we teachers lose track of our students, what has become of them, but the thing that makes it all OK, and keeps life flowing, is when we welcome the new group of eager youngsters through our classroom door, and it is again all worthwhile.

On my passage through the School of Life, I am in and out of class-rooms volunteering, sometimes teaching, always learning. Getting to know the backgrounds, personality traits, and kidness behavior and channel it all into a meaningful learning experience for them is the challenge and the source of celebration when we are all successful in the process.

Today I am sitting in a classroom where the teacher has partnered the students up for an interview process and then the questioning per-son reads to the class the answers of their partner. I learned from the interview responses how rich and diverse is our small group and how we mirror the wider world outside our classroom. Some students have come from other schools, from nearby places or places far away . . . an English-language learner from Portugal, another from Australia, an adopted child from the African continent, a girl whose first name honored the name of her great-great-grandmother; favorite foods, favorite sports, things they like to do after school, and so on. We are just getting started, and where we all take each other is yet to be known, but for sure, we will have a chance to teach and learn from each other, as we move along our individual paths in this classroom setting.

THERE IS A CERTAIN ARTISTRY, a deft personal touch, a pervading tone and method that each teacher carries into the classroom that is unique to them and speaks of their compassion, caring, and dedication to their work among children. Their voice, their written words carry the power of encouragement, enthusiasm, and passion for their chosen life's work.

Their actions and their words speak of inspiring and modeling the highest potential and the unlimited possibilities to their students, showing them higher vistas, longer views, further horizons to which they should aspire.

Each classroom I have entered carries on its walls messages and meaningful phrases put there by teachers to remind students of the form and substance of what is being taught there. One such teacher at the end of the school year removes all the words of wisdom from the classroom's walls and sends them home as gifts from teacher to students. This simple but powerful act of giving inspired and moved me to write the following poem called "Words On My Walls."

Upon these walls are words to know me by…
To remember me by…
They are my passion and my life.
I give them to you now…

Take them home, parade them around the house,
put them on your bedroom walls
As beacon, as banner, as beautiful song…
To inspire, to guide, to enrich you.

Love them as I do…
Love them as I have loved giving them to you
Each day of our togetherness this year.

Take these Words On My Walls
And part of me goes with you.

During my school volunteering years, I have spent time both in the lower elementary and middle school levels. I have now had enough years at the school to have worked with first and second graders whom I am now greeting in sixth grade classrooms. The chemistry between us may have changed, but the dynamics of teaching/learning remain our strong connection. If they judge that I am a source of help in their learning, they will approach me. Additionally, the teachers will thrust into my midst those who are in the most need of help. These I work with through the year to win their confidence so I can get inside their heads and make credible progress with them in their studies, as well as doing some self-image building. My middle school experience has been the most challenging and where I need to show the greatest degree of patience with students. In many ways, they move in and out of being kids and are expected to choose adult-levels of responsibility. It is their slippery slope that I feel needs the most nurturing and guidance to navigate through to adulthood.

I met a man yesterday, be he 83 or 89 years old I know not. He was my elder and it crossed my mind I was looking in the mirror at someone who I portended to be, in some mysterious way, the person who might be the future me. He spoke with enthusiasm on his favorite subjects, mentioned books that inspired him, spoke of wanting to be useful as he was in his previous corporate life, and lit on an avenue of mutual interest when I talked passionately and excitedly of the work I am currently loving to do . . . being in the presence of children in the teaching and learning environment of the School of Life. We parted company and I made a mental note that this could be the beginning of some ongoing relationship . . . a kindred spirit and perhaps most importantly, harbinger of some semblance of my future and a clarion call for me to stay the course and not be the last of the teachers of age to walk among the children, but to coalesce, he and me, as the tipping point for other elders to be ignited in useful service.

CHAPTER 9

Nature

Observations and Lessons Learned
From the World of Nature

"I went to the woods because I wished to live deliberately, to front only the essential facts of life, and see if I could not learn what it had to teach, and not, when I came to die, discover that I had not lived."

— HENRY DAVID THOREAU

"As long as I live, I'll hear waterfalls and birds and winds sing. I'll interpret the rocks, learn the language of flood, storm, and avalanche. I'll acquaint myself with the glaciers and wild gardens, and get as near the heart of the world as I can."

— JOHN MUIR

i n t r o d u c t i o n

n a t u r e

As a youngster growing up, I saw the world of nature through the eyes of one born and raised in a metropolis of several million people. My experiences of nature outdoors consisted mostly of city parks and lagoons where one could fish or stroll within the earshot of busy street traffic and the sight of skyscraper buildings, or forest preserves found some distance away set aside for city dwellers like me. Occasionally our family would also take short excursions into the countryside outside the environs of Chicago.

As time went on, my world widened and as I became a young adult, I took opportunities to see and began appreciating the wonders of nature as it unfolded around me. Still, I never really took advantage of or had much interest in fishing, hunting, mountain hikes, or overnight camping. I was always more at home in the Holiday Inns of the world rather than in a sleeping bag under the stars. But I did have the good fortune to become acquainted with people who appreciated and personified the outdoor lifestyle and all things nature related. And in this way I was able to vicariously live the life, as I saw it, of a free-spirited naturalist. One such genuine, true-to-life, at-home-in-the-wilderness gentleman I have come to know I have personified in this way:

Now comes a man out of the best traditions of the West, multifaceted in his interests, firm in his beliefs, laser-focused, and decisive in his actions, which all mirror precisely in his demeanor and personality, his love of nature. A man who raises no gun or arrow to bow for sport but only for sustenance, who looks upon every sentient being, every forested animal, winged and crawling creature as would a modern day Dr. Dolittle, having an affinity for, a rapport with, a whisperer's touch and a natural kinship and bonding with such creatures. A man who, while walking with you on the trail unfamiliar to you, looks up to the distant mountain peaks and surprises you with a personal recollection of a time in his distant past, when he had cross-country skied over that very mountain right there at the most accessible gap between peaks, and in detail, about his overnight camping experience back then. Put him on an unfamiliar mountain hiking path, and he is at home with all its surroundings, identifying flora and fauna by name as well as by usefulness if one were to be on an extended overnight excursion into the wilds and needed medicinal or nutritional support from Mother Nature.

He has a way of turning his head, listening to his surroundings, and naming the animals and birds making calls and sounds within his hearing. His memory equally captures and recalls his past experiences of trapping, identifying, tagging, and then turning loose bears back into the wilderness, all done under a government program of scientific study he participated in, and, in so telling, names the habits of predators and the tendencies and inclinations of bears under various habitat conditions and situations.

At other times and places, he has plied the water passages in Alaska salmon fishing on large commercial trawlers and when the salmon showed up, recalls the hours and hours of backbreaking and gut wrenching pulling and hauling, straining and sweating until the last of the school of salmon had been depleted, then having to repeat the process at the next salmon sighting.

His love of all things winter-ish has taken him skiing and snowshoeing in various parts of the world, including some of the most arduous slopes and trails in the United States. He has used his love of the outdoors, his enthusiasm, and his communication abilities to inspire others and instill in them outdoor wilderness survival skills and respectful use of natural surroundings.

Now, with having had the good fortune of knowing those who are bonafide naturalists and the opportunity to visit some of the most beautiful places of nature in our land, what follows is my recollected observations and experiences of nature coming into my life, leaving a lasting impression and changing me irrevocably for the better.

*T*he summer is near upon us, the snows have kissed our trees and grassy places for the last time, and old endings say their final good-byes. New beginnings embrace us with new and tantalizing ideas of things both known and unknown yet to come.

Those known are the well-planned-ahead-of-time trips involving planes and rental cars and condos by the beach; mountain getaways and hideaways next to crystal clear placid lake waters, where moose and deer roam the shores, eagles and hawks swoop to catch their dinner, snatching fish from the water, as fish duck and dive under to avoid being a meal; hummingbirds startle as they flutter and fly around feeders placed on porches overlooking the water.

We open our minds almost without notice or effort, and thoughts slip in to touch us, to move us, to gently poke and prod us, into higher realms of used-to-be's or our greater-yet-to-be's, leaving imprints, impressions, and expressions, some shadowy, some concrete, declaratory, affirmative, ready for our right action, all born here in the budding summertime where dreams unfold and memoirs start their journey of unfoldment.

It is ironic and paradoxical to find in the midst of the quietude of life at the beach, signs and signals that jolt you back to reality as you try to slip away and push away your own everyday existence and replace it, if only for a little while, with something called "vacation," vacating your reality, and replacing it with a charming and fantasy-like existence . . . walking squarely into the midst of a beach-side wedding . . . stopped hushed and still, not moving, ears cocked to listen to the minister pronouncing, "You are now husband and wife." Then it's over, and we go on about the business of vacation . . . .

Again while on the beach, startled by two young men running frantically from a crowded beach pavilion, something in hand, slamming themselves into the back seat of a waiting car and speeding away. Men, women, startled faces, angry and belligerent, a beautiful day at the beach, literally stolen from them along with prized possessions. Yes the contrasts of good and evil are here to be found even in paradise. Reality of life is always in motion, happening all around us, even while on vacation.

In the land of paradise, wide horizons, vast vistas of miles and miles of sky meeting beach, waves kissing shore, sunshine blessing each and every diamond and pearl of land and sea it looks upon and touches . . . there is an undercurrent of life, of activity, of planning and doing, of letting go of old and basking in the pleasure of the new. . . . And flowing through this picture of paradise found is the rhythm of days and weeks spent, seasons coming and going, years trundling by. . . . time passing and the landscape, seascape, promontory, and plains remain unmoved, unwithered, seemingly untouched in this, our one and only lifetime of existence. May we be ever vigilant to be awake and aware, to see clearly the nuances, the subtleties, the fine features, and the distinctions of the changing scene before us. Though some of it seems immovable to the eye, follow the seasons of summer, fall, winter, spring, rainy, hurricane, turtle hatching—seasons all, fold it all into your experience and live the larger life.

It is ironic but seems appropriate to reflect on our time in paradise and recall the book by Marianne Williamson called *A Return to Love,* in which she admonishes us to consider "the practice of love as a strength, as a daily answer to the problems that confront us, a guide to the miraculous application of love as a balm on every wound."

Good thoughts carried with us on our beach walks and celebratory meals with friends. And at the end of paradise ascending, now to descend, wrap up, pack up, finish up all the thoughts of ending this visit, going from school year ending, paradise receding, sunsets disappearing, good-bye to friends well-met . . . to close the door as another door opens . . . taking us into new ways of seeing our relationship to the world, to our health habits, to our servant leadership roles to those, both known and not yet known to us, awaiting our "yes" and "amen" to new ways of going and being to other sentient beings who come into our life. What we have learned of ourselves here in paradise we take with us to prosper us, to bless our activities, to sanctify our souls.

EVERYWHERE AMONG THE INTERMOUNTAIN regions and peaks of the Rocky Mountains there is on display the celebration of the human spirit through the outdoor activities that abound on every trail, on every country roadway, in every park, on every accessible and nearly accessible mountain peak. What calls these beings of nature to want to run harder, bike further, climb higher, amidst the grandeur of nature's splendiferous display of flora and fauna, rocks and rills dotting the countryside? One more mile, one more mountain peak, one more road to travel . . . calling to one's indomitable spirit to strive and achieve, to enjoy the process and when accomplished to seek more of the same elsewhere. In the words of the Dan Fogelberg song: "The higher you climb, the more that you see. The more that you see, the less that you know. The less that you know, the more that you yearn. The more that you yearn, the higher you climb. The farther you reach, the more that you touch, the more that you touch, the fuller you feel. The fuller you feel, the less that you need, the less that you need, the farther you reach." Whether it be spiritual growth, personal fulfillment, creating a useful life, we pray to receive it.

Consider the hummingbird that inhabits the alpine forests surrounding mountain lakes and streams, seemingly in the midst of all that this tiny bird would ever need. Now comes Mr. Copper, a hummingbird of brilliant bronze color, larger than most, and should we sit still and quietly watch, he has a lesson to teach us. By his flittery movements and antics we see he is trying to keep all others away from the sugared-water bird feeders that hang from the porches of every vacationer's log cabin—by the hundreds, it seems. Mr. Copper spends his days and nights attempting to keep all others away from the feeders, and there are dozens of his kind to deal with; impossible task, but he keeps trying. Does Mr. Copper not know that there is enough for everyone and that he could not possibly need all that he is hoping to protect and keep from others?

Should we ourselves look around and see what we have accumulated and come to value, holding it closely to ourselves, expending our energies, becoming our thoughts, creating our words, actions, habits, our values . . . and ultimately our destiny? Do they serve our best interests, our spiritual soul-selves?

If, for instance, you were hiking and at the crest of the high point of a hill, you looked down and saw the most pristine, resplendently tree-lined, silvery smooth-surfaced lake of breathless beauty, would you be in a hurry to be somewhere else, to be looking for the fastest way across and be on your way? Instead, if you were hungry and resourceful you might be thinking of a way to catch some fish and assuage your appetite. If you were tired you might just lay in the grass and contemplate the passing clouds and the serenity of the area. If you wished to memorialize the experience, you might pull a writing journal out of your backpack and jot down a few paragraphs for safekeeping of this moment. If you had come from an urban setting, you might consult a map for the nearest town or sign of civilization.

QUANTUM THEORY INTRODUCES US to a universe full of possibilities and probabilities, and it is how you perceive the physical attributes around you that creates your world of reality and motivates you into action or reflection. Are you ready to create a world of dreams?

Perhaps you have a place in mind, a magical place of memories, of hopes created and hopes fulfilled. A place of family bonding, of friendships renewed and made anew. Perhaps it is a place, both physically beautiful but restful to the soul as well, made of mountain streams and lakes, hummingbirds and alpine forest, of swooping birds catching fish over silvery-smooth waters but also made, in the mind's eye, by more wistful and esoteric images created by experiences at other times, in other places . . . but this place, this current and immediate place, brings all the past telescoping into the present, combining and energizing past experiences with dreams yet to be manifested, yet to materialize, even yet to be dreamed. "Place" is where you are, where you have been, and where you are yet to be. If we grow where we are planted, our dreams will wait on future events to find us and fulfill all that we desire and have wished for.

Should you spent more than a little time observing the workings of nature, while sitting beside an alpine-blanketed mountain lake . . . you might see the extremes of nature working their way out in the daily activities of the hummingbird and the moose. The hummingbird darting, hovering in mid-air, whirring and whirling, hurtling through space, territorial and competitive, fighting over sugared-water containers hung from porches of vacationer's log cabins . . . and the moose slow and lumbering, grazing on soft grass, reaching into trees for succulent leaves, plodding through cooling lake shoreline waters, seemingly without other animal predators, anchored and wedded to the Earth on which they move and get their sustenance, occasionally lying in the shade with ears like antenna keeping "sound watch" while the rest of their bulk lay in leisure until hunger prompts them to move on. The hummingbird and the moose, worlds apart in demeanor and physical attributes but sharing a common ground for living and surviving in nature's paradise.

THE BEACH IS LIKE A metaphysical place of being, a sanctuary in the church of all-inclusion, welcoming the most diverse, differentiated, and dissimilar that humanity could possibly put together in one place at one time. There is room for all to be who they are in a way that no other place can offer. There is every gender, age, color, from every corner of our land and beyond our borders.

I have seen with my own eyes the creativity and imagination displayed up and down the beach in the wide variety of athletic endeavors like circle volleyball, paddleball, hands moving as if playing a video game, kite surfing, parasailing, boogie board surf riding, playing soccer and football and baseball. Artistic displays of sand sculpting from the most sophisticated to the basic offerings of children are to be seen everywhere along the water's edge. My heart was warmed as I observed not only children (of all ages) but autistic individuals and the Alzheimer's afflicted being helped into the water to enjoy a buoyant ride on the waves, which their bodies would not have allowed them on land. The sea and the beach could only have been created by a Divine Intelligence sharing its loving-kindness with us humans.

Any keen observer of the habits of the heron will know that most times they can be seen solitarily at the water's edge or in low flight over shallow water, ever in search of grubs or sea anemone-type creatures. Sometimes in twos and threes but no more . . . except when you come across them at around three or four o'clock in the afternoon, gathered by the dozens, webbed-feet in shallow water, each gazing stock still out to sea as if each had been given the message that "school" had been let out for the day and the fish therein were now loose and near shore, or the ice cream truck were about to arrive . . . so be prepared. It looks for all intents and purposes like a "heron happy hour."

Random thoughts emerge along crystalline beaches that stretch as far as the eye can reach. Shell-strewn pieces tossed from the sea, light and bright, all a-glittery, are there for the taking. And in the sky, nature's wonderland of animal menageries captures drifting poodle-like patches of clouds and a Scottie, too. A long-necked swan-shape wisp of a cloud can be seen briefly in the cloud mist, and then let go, not to persist or stay.

Folks ply the beach for trivial pursuits and treasure, beachcomber, vacationer, fortune hunter, storyteller. Tents cluster, like cities springing up against the sun, some welcoming its sun-tanning rays but others shielding against its searing heat. Tricky is the balancing act between pleasure and pain, only several degrees of separation between sunburn and suntan, boon or bane. And if one may be so lucky as to find, wedged in the bough of a brambly bush offshore, a seashell curiously fashioned as a mermaid's comb . . . and fain to recall the fable of its being lost and a new one made by the boy from North Uist for his mermaiden, in the "The Mermaid Who Lost Her Comb."

There is a man who appears on the beach, focused and intent on his task. Others around him walk or run or snooze contentedly in their lounge chairs, but he plies his trade of combing the beach for treasure, seemingly oblivious to the activity or inaction of those around him. His life is like a game of lottery where, should he make the right move, be in the right place, be the luckiest man on earth . . . he would then vanish never to be seen again on the beach but be transported to some other more exotic or exciting locale more to his liking where he may or may not have to continue his daily activity, as he chooses. But here on this beach, he must ever follow his inner calling, hoping for the big strike, ever optimistic, relentless, persistent. He follows the time-honored tradition of those who have gone before him. He stands apart from all the rest on the pristine patch of beach, a man on a mission, the symbol of hopefulness and high anticipation to land the big one . . . for he is the image of a beachcomber, steadfast in his work, sparingly rewarded with occasional success.

CHAPTER 10

Love

Getting Lost in What I Love To Do

"We need to expand our sense of spiritual responsibility beyond the confines of our own lives. If we are here to love, that means not only our children, but also the children on the other side of town and the other side of the world."

— MARIANNE WILLIAMSON

"Love cannot remain by itself — it has no meaning. Love must be put into action, and that action is service."

— MOTHER TERESA

"Some day, after we have mastered the winds, the waves, the tides, and gravity, we shall harness . . . the energies of love. Then for the second time in the history of the world, we will have discovered fire."

— PIERRE TIELHARD DE CHARDIN

i n t r o d u c t i o n

l o v e

    Whenever and wherever we begin to see our place in the world, in sacred ritual, through ceremony or in solitude, we end up laser-focused on sacred service to the one in need who stands before us. If we are comfortable within an institutional setting that provides us purpose, sociability, companionship, meaning, identity, a self-naming mechanism for who we are, and an outlet for our innermost urges to serve, to be useful, to matter, it then translates and transforms into a tangible connection, embracing and embodying the people around us. We start with a living idea, urged on by inner purpose, and we create outcomes that change those whom we have come to know and to love in the deepest sense of Agape love.

L *ove is all around, sometimes in disguise, sometimes boldly shouting out: "Here I am; I've been waiting for you. We have work to do in the world, work that only you and I together can do . . . that which we have been called to do. Let's begin!"*

I keep my eyes and heart open, awake and aware, for signs and signals of voids and open spaces that need to be filled with love. I keep myself at the ready, primed and patient, prepared to be vulnerable, open, cooperative and willing . . . an instrument of love for Spirit to use, and in my being used, I am enhanced, made whole, spiritualized, and energized into my power and my greatest good.

The first thing that must happen is that one must love oneself, and this takes great courage in the face of a diminished self-worth, a focus on lack and limitation, limited vision of how one is reflecting to others in our world. We see our shortcomings first and many times their shadows on our thoughts stop us and hold us back from seeing the essential good inside our soul-selves. It is a blessing and an act of love when others celebrate us and hold a mirror before us, showing us the truth of who we are and how our greatest good makes a difference in the world. If your love is hiding, call it out into the light so the world can be a little brighter for those around us. Love yourself enough to let go of those thoughts and things that do not serve you. It all starts with this intentional act of self-love.

ONE OF THE HARDEST THINGS to convince yourself of as you live your life is that you deserve to be happy. When you are always working hard to please others and pushing your own needs and wants deeper and deeper inside that dark space called "little me," your happiness can only be achieved from the outside, and that outside approval comes and goes, waxes and wanes, blows hot and cold . . . with the passage of time, of people in and out of your life, with the movement and change in circumstances and situations we all face on a daily basis. Isn't it exhausting and futile to follow rules and standards that keep moving and changing and that bring angst and fear and disappointment every time they show up? . . . and they show up often and sometimes with a vengeance. The place to reside in peace and quietude is within your own soul-self, which always is true to you, celebrates you, raises you up, values you highly, and is reliable and trustworthy to lead you home. You can relax now, for you are home.

Would it not be the perfect culmination of one's life to know that they had loved greatly and that love was complete in them—sweetly, considerately, thoughtfully played out each and every day of one's existence? Would it not be the most pleasing and blissful illumination of thought to realize that one's life had been spent making a loving home, building a welcoming haven, providing a bridge of compassion and caring for those we had met on life's journey, and in the meeting each to each, we and they had been better for such encounter, served well, burdens lightened, friends well-met, hearts enjoined in love expressed? Oh, how joyful would be the sound of a resounding "Yes" to such weighty questions of life's purpose and meaning. At life's end to know that one has run a proper race, been useful to most, not harmful but helpful, to have moved mountains, maybe, but to certainly have planted trees . . . the shade of which I shall never sit under, for sure . . . Such is a proper legacy, perhaps even a lasting one, if one is to think well of oneself.

FORGIVENESS STARTS FROM WITHIN, in the dark recesses of the heart where denials and self-righteousness live; where hands made for meditation and *Namaste* turn to finger-pointing and vindictiveness. Where we dwell among the shadows, stuck and smugly contemptuous and unyieldingly unforgiving. . . . a big hill to climb to get to a place where we can love our brothers and sisters in faith, see things differently, turn self-forgiveness into forgiveness of others and truly change the world for the better. As Lewis B. Smedes encourages us, "You will know forgiveness has begun when you recall those who hurt you and you feel the power to wish them well."

Let us take courage and soulful direction from the forgiveness of our wider world, as modeled by such thought leaders and way-showers as Jesus, Nelson Mandela, Mahatma Gandhi, Martin Luther King Jr., and Viktor Frankl, among others. One will sleep better at night knowing that one's authenticity and congruity both inside and outside have been restored, preserved, and circulated as God's givingness, reflected in our loving-kindness to all of God's children.

If we are to experience higher realms of happiness and deeper connection to those we have come to love and cherish, we must forgive ourselves for having moved on, for having left behind those who, through fate or fortune found elsewhere, have gone on, through transition from this world or through incompatibilities or differences unresolvable have grown us apart ... and so each moves on. Signs and signals begin to show up, beckoning us to let go of any pain from the past, to see ourselves and the world around us in new positive and welcoming ways.

We start living life on the lighter side; we begin to attract people to us who have a high degree of compatibility and connectivity to what we believe in and what we stand for. It all starts with self-forgiveness ... when you have lost a dear loved one and you feel guilty you were the survivor, or when you find true and lasting joy and happiness while so much suffering and neediness surrounds you ... then you must be the beacon of hope, the sacred strength, the modeling to show just how good life can be.

Epilogue

Destiny Beckons... What's Next?

*U*pon entering my eighth decade of life, I was gifted with the discovery deep within my personal notes, a cache of carefully concocted continuous streams of creative consciousness interspersed with some revved up ramblings, which now has become the book you have before you.

This exercise in self-discovery, this awakening of awareness of my gifts and talents, has now evolved into my daily practice of illuminating and exploring other paths of literary potential, of commercial value or otherwise, and in so opening myself to it, I have used the technique of naming myself, or observing in the ways others have named me, that create uniquely my own identification and provide insight and impetus for my task that would fit the rigors of my literary journey: thusly, I have identified myself in the context of: wordsmith, writer of poetry, spell-binder, observer, facilitator, questioner, scribe, jokemeister, laser-focused, kinesthetic learner, sage on stage, guide on the side, outlier, hero, renaissance man, revealer, discerner, self-actualized, child whisperer, witness, servant leader.

The Zen Buddhist master Thích Nhất Hạnh puts "naming" this way:

"Every time we call something by its name,
we make it more real,
like saying the name of a friend."

My mind is a workbench and toolbox of words, phrases, ideas, and creative imaginings, which is currently pondering and preparing material such as can be put into children's books—descriptive personas of people I admire, poems, affirmations, commentaries on life, and the like.

May I now close with a quote from Rumi, a 13th century Sufi mystic:

"Out beyond ideas of wrongdoing and rightdoing
there is a field. I'll meet you there.
When the soul lies down in the grass the world
is too full to talk about."

Perhaps this book is our beginning, yours and mine, a meeting place in a field of our thoughts conjoining to create a spirit of right action that makes the world a better place for those around us; and as we think, act, and become a life well-lived, perhaps we shall meet again in another field of our existence, a nirvana that enfolds us as a "transcendent state in which there is neither suffering, desire, nor sense of self, no cycle of death and rebirth," our vision quest clearly set out before us.

N a m a s t e

About the Author

Roger T. Berg

Roger was born and raised in Chicago, Illinois, and lived there until graduating from high school. At age eighteen, Roger joined the U.S. Army and spent three years in the Finance Corp. at various duty stations, including overseas in France. Roger graduated from Michigan State University and holds a degree in Economics from Honors College.

He spent the next thirty-six years in the energy industry in public utility electric and gas distribution and uranium subsidiary asset utilization and disposition, working in treasury cash management, finance, and accounting until his retirement.

Answering the call to volunteerism, Roger has spent the last twelve years in the elementary school environment, teaching and learning language arts and mathematics while promoting the appreciation of great books, language arts, and creative writing and thinking. As a lifelong learner, Roger has come to appreciate the rich traditions and treasure trove of literature and philosophical thought available to ponder and learn from.

He has been recognized for his school volunteerism by receiving the 2009 Heart of Broomfield – Senior Award; being nominated for the 2011 Heart of Broomfield – Education Award; receiving the 2013 Home Instead Senior Care Senior Service Award for Colorado; and having the Aspen Creek School PTA Volunteer of the Year Award named after him.

Roger lives in Broomfield, Colorado, with his wife Joyce, a constant supporter and advocate for his literary endeavors.